My Life With A Cop

How to Survive the Ride

Ruth Verbree

My Life With A Cop
How to Survive the Ride

Published by
10-10-10 Publishing
Markham, Ontario
CANADA

ISBN 13: 978-1530149810

Kamloops, BC, Canada
Www.mylifewithacop.com
E: ruthverbree@shaw.ca

For information about special discounts for bulk purchases, please contact 10-10-10 Publishing at 1-888-504-6257

Printed in the United States of America

Contents

How to Survive the Ride

1. Be in love with the person, not the uniform.
2. Look at every challenge from a positive perspective.
3. Walking and talking.
4. Letting go.
5. Doing things together that you both enjoy.
6. Have your own identity.
7. Hit the storms of life head on.
8. Allow yourself time to grieve.
9. Leaning on Faith.
10. Support one another and have fun.

Dedicated to my Mom: Best Friend, Wife, Mother, Grandmother, Great grandmother, Friend and Mentor (April 20, 1937 – April 17, 2014)

Dear Mom,

I dedicate this book to you, because I am the woman that I am today because you loved me unconditionally and believed that I could do anything I set my mind to. You gave me an example to follow and taught me the golden rule: Do unto others as you would have others do unto you. I look forward with anticipation to the day we meet again; until that time – I love you, Mom.

She is Gone

You can shed tears that she is gone, Or you can smile because she has lived, You can close your eyes and pray that she will come back, Or you can open your eyes and see all that she has left, Your heart can be empty because you can't see her, Or you can be full of the love that you shared, You can turn your back on tomorrow and live yesterday, Or you can be happy for tomorrow because of yesterday, You can remember her and only that she is gone, Or you can cherish her memory and let it live on, You can cry and close your mind, be empty and turn your back, Or you can do what she would want:, smile, open your eyes, love and go on.

David Harkins

Acknowledgements

I would like to personally thank my husband who encouraged me to fulfil my dream of writing this book. Without him, "My Life With A Cop" would never have come to pass. We have lived a dream, are still living the dream and have been called "the Power Couple." I love you dearly, Robert.

I would like to thank Bernice Maude Verbree, my mother-in-law, for the support and love she has shown me throughout the years even though the many miles separated us. Thank you for the gift of your son and for encouraging him to live out his dream, which included me, even though it meant letting him go. You taught him well and brought him up to not only respect men, but also respect women who think for themselves, for which I am truly grateful.

I would like to thank my three children and their spouses for the countless joy they have brought to my life. I am proud of each of you and love the way you have grown into the men and women you have become. The world is a better place because of each of you. I love you with all my heart.

I would like to thank my family and friends, from all the different places we have lived, for the input you have had in my life. You are all blessings from God and I thank Him for allowing you to be a part of my life.

More importantly, I thank Mr. Raymond Aaron, NY Times Top 10 Bestselling Author, my personal Mentor and Coach, and his team for assisting me with my book.

There are many more people I could thank, but time, space, and modesty compel me to stop here.

About Ruth

Awarded the Authority In Aspiring Entrepreneurs by New York Times Best Selling Author Raymond Aaron, Ruth is an aspiring business woman who is seeking to help spouses of first responders, by sharing her own real life examples of overcoming challenges and celebrating victories. Her desire is to help spouses of first responders by empowering them through her experiences and depth of knowledge.

The author currently lives in Kamloops, British Columbia, Canada, with her retired husband, ex-RCMP officer and lives close to her children and grandchildren. They are currently running a little coffee shop in downtown Kamloops, where their day to day lives are affecting the lives of their customers in a positive way. Ruth and her husband have hopes and dreams of helping their community in much more substantial ways and, therefore, are seeking to build and transform their online business to help reach this goal.

Ruth has worked in many different industries throughout her lifetime including being a stay-at-home mother, working in sales, the service industry, as a special needs support worker, to working online and being the owner operator of a few different businesses.

With this book, she has shared her years of experience and her journey through the ride of her life with a cop or a first responder. She has found that there is a genuine need for support for people going through these rough times of PTSD or operational stress injury with their partners. Ruth and her husband, Robert, have survived this ride together, difficult as it was. They endeavor to reach out to others and in some way be able to help them move forward through their stressful time due to being a first responder of serious incidents.

Currently Ruth owns and operates multiple ventures within her corporation and through her portfolio of online platforms. www.mylifewithacop.com | www.PTSDbattleplan.com

Foreword

Have you ever thought about your life purpose? Like most people, you probably have not. Have you ever thought that it was time to transform your life, but never knew how? You probably have lots of things you love doing, many things you want to experience, goals you want to achieve and a dream of an extraordinary life. Again, if you are like many people, your life is filled with activities, obligations and commitments that have nothing to do with your goals or your dreams. You may be spending your life running faster and faster trying to keep up and at the same time falling further and further away from living that extraordinary life about which you are dreaming.

When we meet someone who has transformed their life, they always seem more interesting, more engaging. They have a renewed energy, they are passionate about their work, about life and, in general, about everything. To transform your life takes time, passion, courage and a lot of self-awareness.

Ruth is someone who has definitely overcome a life-changing event and found a way into her own transformation. When she speaks you can sense that she has turned her life around; when you hear her speak you know there is something different, something resonates, what she is saying is true, even though you may not have heard it expressed in that way before. Her passion is to help those less fortunate than her to realize their dreams and goals and to help recovering first responders and their spouses get their lives back on track, living their life purpose, being happy doing it and feeling extraordinary.

In this book you will find simple life examples, experiences and suggestions that you can follow that will empower you to live an exceptional life with a first responder. Start applying this now and move towards an extraordinary life. I'm sure there are many ideas and suggestions in this book that will resonate with you.

Raymond Aaron
NY Times Bestselling Author

Introduction

I had a wonderful childhood. I grew up in central British Columbia in the small town of Vanderhoof, with a population of approximately 5000 people. There were not a lot of street lights, not a lot of anything going on but a great place for a child to grow up. I had a lot of freedom. My parents were happily married throughout my childhood and I grew up with really not a care in the world. I had a home that was warm and loving and I was an easygoing, carefree kid. I was clothed and fed and had every need met. I was a privileged child and enjoyed a lot of extras in my life such as horseback riding, skidooing, skiing, minibiking, swimming and was roaming freely without having to worry about harm. My home life was stress-free and my school life was filled with activities that I thoroughly enjoyed.

As I grew older, my activities changed from roaming the hills and building forts to dating, going out for drives and coffee, and eventually falling in love! I was infatuated at an early age and my boyfriend and I became best friends. We had a wonderful couple of years together through high school, which changed my thinking from wondering what I was going to do in life to thinking that I would just get married and have a house with a white picket fence and live happily ever after.

Then one day my only brother set me straight by making me really consider how ridiculous I sounded. How would I even consider getting married at 16 and how would I manage to make ends meet. After contemplating how I really felt, I realized that my inner adventurous spirit would be trapped if I actually did get married and settle down so young. This set me on a completely different path and I decided to leave the little town I knew and loved. I headed out to a place 1000 miles away from home, to a private high school that I had heard about, to try and figure out what I really wanted out of life. At the age of 17, with tears of sorrow and excitement, I said goodbye to my loving but supportive parents, my boyfriend who I intended to marry after grade 12, and my best girl-friend in the world with whom I shared every secret a girl could have. I left with a cousin of mine and we made the 2-day trek across the provinces to the little town of Caronport, Saskatchewan, with only our clothes, bedding and a few personal items.

I lived in an old army base dorm that was converted to a girls' high school wing, and had to share a room with another girl whom I had never met. I had no sisters, only one brother, so sharing was a new concept to me. I lived on a floor filled with other girls my age who came from all over Canada and other parts of the world. At first, this place felt so desperately desolate and I was extremely lonely for my girlfriend and boyfriend, and I longed for my home and my Mom and Dad.

It wasn't too long before this new adventure slowly creeped into my very being and I made friends quickly and enjoyed my new life. I knew that there was more to my life than getting married at the age of 16 and just staying in the little town I grew up in. I had a sense of awakening that would take me through the next years of my life.

You have to know that growing up in the cultural background I was raised in, being a woman, deciding to leave on my own and move so far from home, was not the norm. I was thinking outside of the box, which made me realize that I was different from others in my community in that I really could think for myself.

Before long I fell in love, once again, with another guy who I just thought the world of. I thought he was the true love of my life and that once we both finished college and had our education completed, we would start our lives together and live happily ever after. After a few years in this relationship, I realized that certain things would never change and that I would have to break off this relationship if I ever wanted to move on with my true spirited life. I was ready to go on to the next phase in my adventure and he wasn't, so I let go and decided to move forward with my life. This experience and life event was very hard for me and I didn't realize how much this would affect the rest of my life, in good and bad ways. I was trying to fall out of love and, I believe, this experience might have been what saved me from "Scarlet Fever" (also in the chapters ahead).

In trying to move on with my life, I went back to the town I grew up in and started working in the bank as a teller. I love people and the service industry so this seemed like a good fit for me. Soon I got involved in a bank training program and was on my way to working up the ladder of success.

As I was training, I met a man in uniform (which I will talk about in the first chapter), and to make a long story short, who I ended up marrying. My father, who is very big on commitment, essentially is the man I credit to My Life With A COP! Without his strong characteristic of commitment, our first date would not have happened and a missed opportunity would have changed the trajectory of my life. Thus I call our first date the "Commitment Date." Thank you Dad, for your strong character of integrity and commitment, and for your support to me now and always. I Love You Dad.

Chapter 1
Do You Drive A Yellow Car?

Meeting in the Bank

It was a typical day in the life of the bank but my life was about to do a 180 degrees turnabout without me even knowing it.

I was on a training program through the bank which was going to allow me to move up the ladder of success. I was working diligently at the side counter, when suddenly I heard this voice calling out to me – "Are you Ruth Martens?"

"Yes," I replied, as I looked up into the face of an RCMP officer. I didn't tremble, being only 21, but wondered how he knew my name and what he wanted from me.

"I need to talk to you, so when is a good time?" he asked, "and do you drive a yellow car?"

Now I did drive a yellow car – but what did that matter to him! – is what went through my head.

"Yes I do, and I work until 5 so I guess after that," I answered him back. I was busy, so just kept on working, as he seemed to be in a bit of a hurry too.

"There was a pedestrian hit and run and a yellow car was seen at the scene, so I am following up on leads with people who drive a yellow car. I need to do a quick interview with you about it," he stated. "What's your number?" he threw out at me.

My response was short and to the point, "It's in the book!"

He was okay with that and told me he would call me later, as he could see I was busy and he was kind of in a hurry as well.

My day went on as usual, and I wondered a few times throughout the day why he would need to speak with me, as he clearly knew I wasn't the person who hit the pedestrian. In my mind I figured it was an excuse to phone and ask me out, after all, I was a single blond girl working behind the counter of the bank that he dealt with, but I had no desire to go out with him.

After dinner that night, I received a phone call from none other than the RCMP officer at the bank. I answered a few of his questions and, of course, I hadn't been anywhere near the accident scene. As soon as he got the information he needed from me, he could have said good-bye, but it seemed he wanted to talk to me and I knew he was going to ask me out!

Minutes later I heard his question coming at me, "How would you like to go to a movie with me on Saturday night? We could drive into Prince George, catch the early show, get some dinner and then drive home."

"No thanks, I replied, "I don't even know you and I don't usually date people I don't know."

"It'll be a good time," he persisted. "We'll just catch a movie and drive home."

I thought that it couldn't hurt for me to accept, after all, he should be a respectable guy being a police officer and all. Maybe it would be good for me to get out, so I accepted graciously wondering why on earth I was saying yes. While saying yes to the date over the phone, I had forgotten that I was already going camping for the weekend with family and friends to go swimming and waterskiing, which I loved!

Friday night came and I headed out to the lake forgetting about my "Saturday night date" that I didn't really care to go on. I was still hurting from a break-up and had no desire to get to know another male companion and make small talk.

Friday night and Saturday we had a lot of fun at the lake, swimming and waterskiing, then late in the afternoon I realized that if I was going to go to the movie with this police officer Saturday night, that I soon needed to head home. Just then, some more of my friends drove in to camp for the night. I made a quick decision that I would just let my parents answer the phone when the officer called and tell him that I had decided to stay at the lake and couldn't make the date.

Now the one thing my father did not approve of was breaking a commitment that had been set. When I told him that I didn't really want to go out with this policeman and that they could just tell him I was at the lake, my father replied with "You told him you would go, so you better fulfil your commitment and go."

Dads have a way of making their daughters feel compelled to do certain things and even though I really didn't want to go out on a date this particular evening, I knew that I would disappoint my Dad too much if I didn't keep my commitment. Because of this, my whole life direction changed that night.

I left the lake and got ready for my date. Of course the unpardonable thing happened next! The phone rang and I thought to myself – he's going to phone and cancel the date now after I left my friends and all the fun I could have had at the lake. Sure enough! I answered the phone and heard – "Plans have changed. I forgot that I was invited to an RCMP staff dinner party at a friend's house tonight and I really can't miss it. So how about you come to the dinner party with me first, and then we will head out for the movie after that?"

Now for sure I wasn't going to go to an RCMP staff dinner party where they were all going to inspect me to see if I was good enough for this RCMP member to go out with!

"No, I don't think I want to do that," I said, "That's okay, you just go to your dinner party."

He wouldn't take no for an answer though and after telling him that I didn't want his whole office inspecting me, he said they wouldn't do that. He said they were all such nice people, the food would be so delicious and I would be missing out on a very good time if I didn't go etc. etc. blah, blah, blah. I finally caved in and said okay, I would go.

Soon the doorbell rang and Constable Verbree was at the door to pick me up.

Opportunities always come our way but so often we tend to miss them or pass them by, not realizing that they could change our course of direction.

Rebound Date

As I got into his little 240 Datsun, my fears abated a little, only to resurface as we entered the door to the party. So many policemen, all wondering who Verbree was with this evening. I expected to at least be able to sit with Robert, called Bob because there were 3 cops with the name Robert at this detachment, but to my dismay the hosts made sure the guests were all seated with someone other than their partner this evening.

The meal was very delicious, home-made Chinese food, and after some polite small talk and an amount of time so as not be rude, we said our good-byes and headed into PG to watch a movie and have our "date."

We had a nice time out together and our conversation turned to what we both had in common - our recent breakups from past relationships. Bob had been engaged previously and had just recently received the ring back in the mail. I had previously broken off a long-term relationship from which I was still grieving. We chatted about why an RCMP officer like him would ask out a small town girl like me, especially since I had a strong faith in God which he himself did not share. I had a strong cultural background with such large family ties and Bob was from the other side of the country, Newfoundland to be exact! We seemed like the two most unlikely people to ever be together but we had a nice time that evening. When we said our good-byes I thought I would never see him again and that wouldn't really matter to me. I was not heart struck, nor uniform struck, I did not have "Scarlet Fever," nor did I wish to have a relationship with this Mountie. Scarlet fever was a term used, by members in the RCMP, when someone fell in love with the Red Serge uniform and this certainly did not pertain to me.

The Commitment Date was over and I could be rest assured that my father was proud of me for sticking to this commitment. On returning home that night, I told my parents that we had a lot in common and could relate to each other because of our recent breakups, but that he really just needed someone to talk to about his ex-fiancée breaking up with him.

The Axe and the Big Question

It was a few weeks later in September that Bob phoned me out of the blue and asked me out for a coffee date. I assumed it wouldn't hurt to have coffee together so we made the arrangement to meet. We met at a truck stop in town for coffee and got caught up on the last few weeks of life. He had just seen his parents, who had flown out from Newfoundland to see where their son was living, and I had just recently accepted a transfer within the bank to continue my training and was moving an hour and a half west of Vanderhoof to train in another branch in Burns Lake. I would be coming home on the weekends and just living in a hotel during the week. He seemed okay with me leaving because I was pursuing a career with the bank but asked if he could continue seeing me and that he would drive out for dinner the following week.

Through October and November we continued to see each other sporadically and we realized that we had quite a lot in common. We were beginning to build a friendship and who knew where this would take us. I still was not infatuated but I did enjoy the comradery and knew that this Newfie would definitely broaden my horizons. I was a girl who was open to adventure so that certainly intrigued me.

Winter came and my little yellow Dodge Colt was handling just fine in the snow with me driving back and forth to Burns Lake, even though sometimes I had to follow the plow trucks to make it home to Vanderhoof. One weekday evening in somewhat of a snow storm, Bob drove out in his old Chevy truck to see me. We had dinner together but then suddenly he started getting all personal and wanted to talk about getting married. I had known him for about 3 months now and had only seen him on the weekends and occasionally once during the week. This particular evening, however, he wanted to talk about marriage and get very personal. I wasn't ready to talk about marriage but more than that, I just knew I couldn't marry a man that didn't share my personal faith. As we kept talking, I eventually said that I knew we could have a marriage that might survive if we never had children, but that if we were to have children, I would want to bring them up in the faith that I had been raised in. I really didn't think that a marriage would survive not being united in this way, so I said that I would not marry him in this present situation. That night he decided he would start to attend church with me and said that he wanted to change his life, but was this for real or was he just saying this for me? How could I tell?

By now the mild snow storm had turned into quite the blinding snowstorm, but Bob still left for Vanderhoof in his old white Chevy truck after this long heavy conversation. He said he would be fine, as he had to go to work the next morning and he had rescue packs in his truck if anything went wrong. He had a skidoo suit to keep warm, gloves and a hat, a pick-axe, and a shovel, so he should be okay. He was a good driver and a strong young man so we said our good-byes and I would see him on the weekend.

At about 2 in the morning I was startled by a pounding on my motel door and someone calling out to me. I slowly went to the door and asked who was there. My heart was beating with fear wondering who would be at my door at 2 in the morning?

"It's me," yelled Bob, the words coming out garbled and slow, "it's me!"

I reluctantly opened the door and the sight was somewhat frightening, like something out of a movie! There was Robert wearing his skidoo suit, toque and mitts and covered with ice and frozen from head to toe. In his hand he held this huge axe; anyone seeing this site would have been horrified. I knew he was a strong young man but not quite this strong! His truck had broken down on the road about 14 miles out of town. He had to walk all the way back to my motel room in the blinding snowstorm because there was no traffic on the roads in this weather to give him a lift. This poor guy; my heart went out to him and right then and there I knew he was a keeper!

Getting Married

Things were moving fast, probably another trait of a type A personality. Did I really love this guy? I was still reeling over the loss of my last relationship. Did he love me? He was still reeling over being dumped from his last relationship and the engagement ring appearing in the mail.

Around the middle of December we went to a Christmas "cop" party, another party where the members were wondering if I would meet the grade for dating an RCMP officer. They were beginning to accept me because they had seen us together a few times now, although I was thought of as a bit of a goody two-shoes for this single RCMP officer. After all, how many other women had been on the dating scene for him in this short span of 3 months?

Everyone was chatting and enjoying the festivities but the two of us were off on our own sitting together on a big reclining chair having a drink, when out of the blue came this question.

"Will you marry me?" The music was playing and the Christmas chatter was infectious. I thought I was hearing wrong so politely asked, "What did you say?"

"Will you marry me?" he repeated.

I smiled inwardly and wondered what my answer would be but out came "Yes I will!" We kissed and laughed and decided we would look at the calendar another day to pick a date for the wedding. I didn't know if this was for real or whether it was just the Christmas cheer we were experiencing and that this conversation would be quickly forgotten. For the moment, it was a wonderful evening to celebrate.

The next few weeks were busy as I was out of town during the week and commuting back home on the weekends. This year was the worst winter for record snowfalls in about 30 years and new records were set. One Saturday in January, the 22nd to be exact, with a foot of snow on the ground and the city snow plow workers on strike, we trucked our way through the streets of Prince George to the different jewelry shops looking for engagement rings. We ended up finding something we liked and by suppertime we had bought our rings. It seemed that the wedding really was going to take place, whether we were in love, in rebound mode, or just for the sake of getting married. We drove up a hill overlooking Prince George, pulled off the road and stopped to see the beautiful lights of the city – and there he asked me to marry him and put the ring on my finger!

The next few months were a blur. I quit my training program through the bank and took a job as the head teller so that we could be in the same place and get to know each other better. Plans emerged and after receiving permission from the commissioner of the RCMP, we were married on May 15, 1982, at 11 a.m. in the Gospel Chapel in Vanderhoof, B.C. Of course there were many challenges in the months leading up to the wedding but we marched forward in spite of this. I was given a lot of advice on why not to marry this Mountie, this man from a different culture, from across the country, this man who didn't share my faith and who wasn't really my type etc. etc. The comforting thing in all of this to me was that my parents both supported my decision to marry this Newfie. They had come to appreciate who Bob was and that he was a genuine man who loved and wanted to take care of their daughter, who respected and loved them both and wanted to be a part of the family and most importantly who wanted to grow in the faith that had become personal for him.

So began the journey of My Life With A Cop.

Fire Crackers in August

I had to decide very early on in my life with this cop that I could not just sit around and worry about when he would be home or how dangerous his job could be, or that he was driving up and down the highway at 200 kilometers per hour, or that he could end up in some fight in a back alley. I had to give away my cares and fears everyday as I prayed that we would be protected from harm. Maybe I was just a bit oblivious as to how dangerous his job really could be until one night in the middle of August. We lived in a little bungalow house only a block from the RCMP station. I worked at the bank and this day was no different from any other day. I came home and made supper but

Bob was late again. When he did arrive home he was full of stories from seizing marijuana from this group of punks in town. These no-good-scum-bag kids were a nuisance and hopefully tonight they had been taught a lesson. After supper he had to go back to the office to do some more paperwork on this drug seizure, so he would be home a bit late.

He was off at midnight and conked in bed soon after he turned out the lights. It had been a busy night. We were both sleeping soundly when suddenly we were startled awake with a loud crashing sound, the sound of 3 bullets being fired, and the smell of gunfire in the air. We liked to sleep in complete darkness, so there were no lights on in the house. Bob always slept with his long-handled flashlight by his bedside (just in case he needed a weapon in the night to protect us with) and everything was locked up tight. This particular night, however, the kitchen window was left open because it had been exceptionally hot and humid this day.

Startled out of a deep sleep, Bob sat up quickly grabbing his flashlight. He told me to stay in bed while he set out to get the attacker. Literally shaking in bed I could see in the darkness where Bob was headed. He snuck down the hall and reached for the light switch ready to attack whomever was there. Realizing soon what had happened, he knew no one was in the house. He was already grabbing for his clothes and the fight was on!

Someone had knocked the kitchen window screen onto the floor causing the loud crashing sound and then had thrown a handful of lit firecrackers into the open window. As the firecrackers blew up, they exploded all the way down the hall close to our bedroom door, filling the house with the smell of gunpowder. There were burn marks on the ceiling, floor and walls which certainly didn't impress the man I married. Bob tore out the door and around the house looking for clues as to who would do this to us. After seeing no one around, he headed for the police station to get the cops on the scoundrel's trail.

Now alone inside, I shuddered to think what could have happened and now understood that life with a cop could be very dangerous. I was just a 22-year-old, naïve, small-town girl who didn't understand how people could be so inconsiderate and live such a different way of life. How would I survive this ride that had only just begun?

Dog Scene in Vanderhoof

Seeing as I wanted to feel a bit safer in my own home in the middle of the night, while my hubby was out keeping the town safe, we decided that a shepherd would be a good fit for the two of us. We found a wonderful pure bread shepherd who became a part of our life and made me feel a whole lot more comfortable alone in the house at night. Bob took great interest in training our dog, Tasha, and she was becoming quite the watch dog. Since shepherds are the breed of dogs the RCMP use for their dog teams, Bob felt that our dog could do some detective work as well. Tasha was a very smart dog and we realized just what a sense of right and wrong she had when late one night at around midnight, she woke us up with her loud barking and growling. She usually only barked for a few minutes if anyone came close to our house, but this particular night she wouldn't stop. Bob got up to check things out but couldn't really see anything. He yelled out the window at her to stop barking and usually she would listen immediately and go back to sleep, but not this moonlit night. She kept on barking and growling until finally we had to bring her inside so as not to wake the neighbours. The persistent growling, teeth showing snarling continued and Bob could see that there was a car parked just down the alley from our house. Since we lived so close to the police station and our dog was acting so much out of character, Bob decided to phone the guys at the station and ask them to check out the car in the back alley. There had to be something unusual going on since Tasha just wasn't settling down.

It was only a few minutes later that the cops were out checking on this vehicle. Bob was out of the house in a flash as well, adrenaline pumping and I was left inside with our shepherd to protect me. The growling abated and soon she was settling down.

Within half an hour, Bob was back as proud as ever to report that our great trained shepherd had just helped bring in two wanted criminals. Not only did she have good reason to growl and bark, she had just helped the RCMP arrest two men with Canada wide warrants. Now that was a satisfying end to an eventful evening! Tasha was definitely smarter than we gave her credit for and I could rest easier at nights knowing that she would protect me if the need arose.

Shirt not Ironed Good Enough

One day Bob was a bit behind schedule for getting to work on time and asked me if I would mind quickly ironing a shirt for him. Naturally, as a young wife, I wanted to help out where I could so I said I would do this for him. I set up the ironing board and started ironing his work shirt. I took great care in pressing the sleeves and spent an extra amount of time making his shirt look fabulous. I had ironed quite a bit in the past, which my Mother had taught me to do quite well, and ironing a shirt was no hard task, I thought!

What I didn't realize though is that police officers are extremely fussy about their police uniforms. Maybe not their civilian clothes but their police uniforms had to be PERFECT! I was doing my best at ironing his shirt but to my horror he took one look at the finished product and said, "I can't wear that - it's just not good enough!"

There was no – "I'm sorry honey" or "Sweetheart, I feel bad to have to say this to you, but the crease is just not sharp enough." Oh no, it was just straight out – "it's not good enough!"

Ironing was definitely not on my list of favourite things to do so right then and there I decided that if my best was not good enough for him, then he could just do his own darn ironing from that day forward and see how he liked that! I didn't realize that such a seemingly unimportant thing would be so utterly important to this Mountie whom I had married. I had never met someone who cared so much about a crease in their shirt, for goodness sake! Was this what life was really going to be like? Were the fine little details of a uniform going to become an issue in our marriage? Who was this crazy man who cared for details like this? I grew up with an entrepreneur Dad who fixed trucks and wrenched all day, who barely had time to eat or sleep let alone worry about a crease in a shirt!

I decided I had to let this one go but realized then that I was married to a "details man" and that we would probably have some disagreements over details in the future. Details are extremely important in many instances, like doing an RCMP investigation for example, but figuring out which details are important and which ones are not life altering, like ironing a crease on a shirt, would be something we would have to work on together. From that day on though, Robert did iron his own shirts and continued to do so throughout his career. In the years that followed he did get a little less obsessive compulsive over the creases in his shirts and sometimes he would even ask for my help if he was running behind schedule. To give Robert some credit here, he definitely was a much better ironer than me and he taught me how to iron the RCMP way, a very valuable lesson indeed.

How to Survive the Ride?

What I realized at a very young age was that to continue on my journey with a cop, I needed to be in love with the person, not the uniform. Going through RCMP Depot, these men and women are brainwashed into thinking that they are a higher class of people and that "Scarlet Fever" is the norm. I knew that not being in love with the "uniform" was a bonus for me, which gave me a different perspective in loving the honorable cops who want to make our country safer. I needed to have a strong sense of commitment regardless of the good and bad, a way to let go of the fear of the unknown, not let the little things become mountains, to be bold enough to state my opinion and know that it mattered, and yet be woman enough to apologize. I had to be open to new things, broaden my horizons, think outside of my culture and live for the here and now. My life with a cop – my love for life – was an action that I committed to not a feeling that came and went, or the ride would have ended way before it was over.

Chapter 2
I'm Never Moving There

The Need to Move!

I mentioned early on that I was related to half the town of Vanderhoof on either my Dad's side of the family or my Mom's side of the family. My parents both came from large families of 8 siblings each and most of them grew up and settled down around the Village of Vanderhoof. The culture I grew up in had very specific traditions and beliefs, one of them being Pacifists, so marrying a cop was a bit over the top for some of my relatives. Carrying a hand-gun that could do damage was a different scenario altogether. Authority figures were very hard for some people to stomach and many of my relatives felt this way about cops in general, not to mention the hard-ass truck-scale authority figures that could make or break the trucker's livelihood. Since "my man" was on highway patrol there were bound to be at least a few scenarios that involved my relatives, either in town or on the highway, that would end not seeing eye to eye with my husband and would come back to me one way or another.

It wasn't long before this started happening. Robert would come home and say, "How is so-and-so related to you? I stopped him on the highway today and he sure wasn't what I would call pleasant! He sure has a bad attitude towards cops!"

I always felt I needed to defend my family but I really don't know why! Robert was only just doing his job and the fact that my relatives didn't want to follow the rules set out by the government – not the police – was not his fault by any stretch of the imagination. He was certainly respectful but, needless to say, I got tired of hearing when I was out and about that the cops in town were awful and what kind of a cop my husband was. People rarely compliment police officers and I was starting to understand why cops would insulate themselves. They live and work in a negative world. It wasn't long before we felt like we really needed to get out of town! Bob was tired of stopping my relatives and being made to feel like he was the "bad guy" and I was tired of hearing about it. We wanted "out!"

Newfie Visit

One night, approximately 9 months into our marriage, we talked about starting a family. We thought we were old enough – I was 22 and Bob was 25 – and many of our friends already had children, so we thought it might be a good idea for us to start a family too. Now, like most young, inexperienced adults, we thought we were ready. Two weeks later the pregnancy test was positive! We were going to be parents whether we were ready or not. We had a little secret which would only be ours for the next few days.

We were scheduled to fly out to St. John's, Newfoundland for our wedding reception with his family since 8000 kilometers had kept almost all his family and friends from attending our wedding ceremony. I had never been to the "rock" before and was looking forward to seeing where this cop I married grew up. I wanted to be able to put a handle on why he was the way he was and learn about his cultural ways and upbringing.

We arrived safe and sound but our little secret didn't remain a secret for too long. I was usually a very energetic, bubbly person but the 4-1/2-hour time difference really did me in. I just couldn't adjust my inner clock and was so tired each day that Robert's mother began to wonder who on earth their son had married. I was referred to as a wilting flower, I remember distinctly, and couldn't eat much and didn't really enjoy sightseeing and driving around the bay. I was car-sick, didn't have the energy to meet new people and certainly couldn't carry on a long conversation without yawning and looking like I was really bored with their company. After a few days of this Robert's mother started suspecting that something was going on – either I was sick or pregnant – but something definitely was going on. Being a nurse for her whole career, his mother was pretty good at figuring things out and thus we had to divulge our little secret.

The reception party did go on as planned and we had a nice celebration. I had to get "screeched in" and "kiss the cod" – all part and parcel of becoming an "honorable Newfoundlander." This culture was so foreign to me and I was learning a lot, despite not feeling my usual self. This was a beautiful, rich island; I just couldn't truly appreciate it for what it was at this time. In the future I would come to fully love "the rock" as so many people do. Having seen and lived where he grew up definitely helped me understand much more about why he talked and acted the way he did. Our childhoods were similar but cultures were very different.

The rest of the visit was a bit of a blur and I barely made it on the plane to get home. I don't know how I survived the 14-hour journey home to Vanderhoof because I was green with nausea and so weak I could barely make it from the terminal to the plane. The excitement of starting a family was beginning to wane as I felt this 9-month flu was never going to end.

First child – Miracle Baby

Everyone told me that I would feel better at the 3-month mark. I kept going to work hoping to feel more energized and get my mind on something else! I had switched jobs since being married and was now working in a school, which allowed me to be home much earlier than working in the bank. I was supposed to have time to prepare dinners and look after my husband like I wanted to, but now being sick with the 9-month flu, I would go lie down and have a nap so that I could survive the evening. Once the school year ended, I didn't go back to work as we had decided that I would be a stay-at-home mom. The budget would be tight but we felt we could do it. I now had time to prepare for a new little person in the house and I could pamper myself and take afternoon naps, the leisurely life with my cop!

Fall turned into winter and before we knew it we were getting ready for Christmas. I loved the Christmas season and this year our little bundle of joy would be our biggest gift. I woke up December 3rd at 1 in the morning and soon realized that this was going to be the big day! By 6 a.m. we were headed to the hospital and by noon we were holding our little miracle child in our arms. What proud parents we were and the first few hours with our new baby daughter were incredibly precious. We just couldn't believe what a miracle it was to give birth to a child and see the tiny fingers and toes that were so adorable and perfect in every way. Our blissful few hours were dampened somewhat when the doctor came into the room and sat down to tell us something we didn't really want to hear.

Our precious little Christmas baby had some heart difficulties, which they couldn't really explain to us very well. They heard heart sounds that were abnormal and swishing noises that shouldn't be heard. Soon all the nurses and doctors were coming into our room wanting to listen to what an abnormal heart beat sounded like in a newborn. The little hospital in Vanderhoof didn't have the right equipment to perform the tests that were needed on an infant. So the doctor explained to us that we would need to go to a tertiary center where the proper tests could be done to determine what was really going on with her heart. They did know, however, that our precious little baby would need heart surgery at some point in her first year of life; fortunately, it just wasn't crucial now.

What a blow to us! She looked perfectly healthy. After the shock wore off and the doctors and nurses all had time to come in and listen to a congenital heart anomaly, we were released from hospital and scheduled to have a doctor's appointment in a week to see how she was doing. At that appointment a week later, we were given the real version of what was going to happen. We would be sent to Children's Hospital in Vancouver, to a heart specialist who would determine the depth of the heart problems she had. Appointments were made and we would be travelling to Vancouver when she was approximately 6 weeks old.

Christmas came and went and our daughter, Cindy Ruth, made Christmas really special for us. Although she was not gaining weight as she should, she was able to nurse well enough and we were getting used to being a family. At 6 weeks of age we were on our way to Vancouver to see the heart specialist. She was seen by two doctors, a pediatric cardiologist and an intern. After numerous tests were performed we were told that she had coarctation of the aorta with a ventricle septic defect (VSD). The VSD was a blessing in disguise as this was allowing some of the blood to escape the narrowing, thus allowing her heart to pump without too much effort. Eventually she would need surgery as this particular narrowing of the aorta never healed on its own. The VSD was about the size of a dime and sometimes these did require surgery and sometimes did not. We were told to go home and would know when it was time to have surgery, when she was turning blue too often, not getting enough oxygen and just not having enough energy to nurse. That was not at all reassuring for first time parents, in fact, it was quite distressing.

Our faith was made stronger through the challenge we were facing and one day while reading the Bible, we felt that we should ask the pastor and deacons of our church to come and pray over our child for healing. This sounded a bit strange to us but we were about to experience something miraculous. We arranged an evening where we gathered together and prayed over our baby for healing. This was quite the experience, very encouraging and uplifting and when we were finished my husband knew in his heart that she was healed.

Some people thought we were absolutely crazy but that didn't matter to us because we knew in our hearts that we were doing the right thing.

For the next few months she continued to thrive and our follow-up appointment in Vancouver had been scheduled for when Cindy was 4 months old. My husband and I were excited to see what the doctors would say and looked forward to what the tests would reveal in a few months' time.

The months flew by and Cindy not only had a bad heart but she was very colicky and had many ear infections. We were tired all the time because of lack of sleep, but surviving parenthood. It wasn't long before our scheduled appointment came and the doctors couldn't believe what they saw on the newly performed tests. There was absolutely no coarctation and all they could really say was that it must not have been there in the first place. We knew differently though as we had seen the pictures previously, and silently we thanked the Lord for our precious miracle child. We knew that God had healed our baby's heart and we were so very thankful. She still had the VSD, but the doctor figured that this would take care of itself and that as she grew the hole would just get smaller in comparison to the growth of the heart. We drove away from the hospital that day knowing that we could only give God the glory. She truly was our miracle child now.

Compassionate Transfer

We felt very relieved knowing that our baby daughter would not need surgery. We still had to see the cardiologist at Children's Hospital every 6 months for a while and then annually until they could release her with a clear heart. Since we had to be down at Children's Hospital twice a year and Robert had already done his time in the small town of Vanderhoof, we asked for a transfer down the Valley to be closer to the cardiologist.

It wasn't too long before we received a compassionate transfer down to Burnaby, BC. I was excited for the chance to live in the big city and experience some real culture. It was a great opportunity to see if we liked the city with just a small child and this was only a 2 to 3 year posting, so we would be gone before she started school. The next day we met with a realtor and our first house went up on the market. The market was slow in 85, interest rates were sky high and we didn't really want to lose money. It was a hard few months realizing that we were going to have to lower our expectations or stay in Vanderhoof.

After months of trying to keep our house clean for showing and bothering our realtor relentlessly, we still hadn't sold our house. We could only defer the transfer for so long as they needed to fill the position in Burnaby, so we had to let the position go. We were then given the options of Abbotsford, Chilliwack or Hope. I was really hoping for Abbotsford or maybe Chilliwack, but certainly I was never moving to Hope!

I'm Never Moving There!

I have since learned never to say never! We really wanted Abbotsford because this was an hour closer to the hospital but we ended up with Hope, of course! We decided that it was time to move regardless of whether our house sold or not, as it was time to leave Vanderhoof. We could always rent our house out if we had to and we could rent an apartment for a while. We were going forward with the move and set out on our first house hunting trip. We found a little apartment to rent for the time being, but also looked at houses to see what the market in Hope had to offer. We fell in love with one house but couldn't afford to purchase it until our house had sold. I was thinking positively and felt that our place would sell at the last minute, so I wasn't letting myself worry about the sale. The moving truck was scheduled and the big moving day was just around the corner. This was it! I was leaving my home town for good, knowing that I probably would never live here again.

The night before the truck was to arrive we had an offer on our house! We had to take a loss but at least we would be free and clear of it and be able to purchase a house in Hope rather than rent an apartment. Robert really wanted a garage to work in and the apartment didn't offer this. Maybe we would still end up with the house we had loved. We finished the last of the paperwork for the sale as the movers were packing up our house and everything was done by suppertime of moving day! What a relief!

A Hard Good-Bye

The next morning we pulled out of Vanderhoof in our little car, the three of us, and headed up the hill out of town. It was definitely emotionally draining leaving so much behind; my fun-loving childhood, Robert's first posting as a cop, our fast romance, our first home, our special watch dog, our miracle child and leaving my loving, supportive parents who meant the world to us.

The adventure ahead was going to be new and exciting but saying good-bye to my parents was the hardest thing in the world. I never dreamt saying good-bye like this would be so difficult. We pulled ourselves together, smiled and kept on driving and focused on what lay ahead – life would be a roller coaster with this cop of mine. There would be no more bubble to live in with family to support me; I would have to pull up my big girl panties now and survive this ride that I had signed up for on my own.

How to Survive the Ride?

Adventures are not always good but if you can look at them from a positive perspective then they generally have a better outcome. Life is constantly changing and in the roller coaster ride of my life with a cop this meant giving up my life in Vanderhoof, my hometown and being able to look at new challenges with an open mind. Some changes would be good and others would be not so good, but there would always be a positive side if I chose to look for it. With buying our first home, getting pregnant and starting a family, living with a child who needed extra care, our commitment to each other took on new meaning. We had both said "I do" for the long term and challenges would either break us apart or make us stand more united. We needed to learn to work together more and look out for each other's interests and needs, in more ways than one.

I believe that having a child with a congenital heart problem and witnessing a miracle in front of our eyes, so early into our marriage, made us bond together in a way that would not have happened otherwise. Getting through the sleepless nights with a colicky child was tough, but this miracle experience and memory to look back on helped to make our marriage stronger right from the start. We have never lost faith in the One who gave us this hope and leaning on our faith carried us through the years to come. To survive the ride I needed to look at every challenge as an adventure and look at it from a positive perspective.

Chapter 3
The Ultimatum!

Are You the Nanny?

Everything worked out with our move just the way it was supposed to. Since our house sold at the last minute we ended up being able to purchase the house we loved. This also prevented us from having to move twice, first into an apartment and then into a house. We moved into a house on Park Avenue close to Kawkawa Lake, a beautiful area of Hope. We lost about $10,000 because of the down turn in the housing market, which was a lot of money back in 85, but gained it on this end. We felt this was the right house to flip and make some money on; it was a 3 bedroom house with a cathedral entrance and the basement was unfinished, so our plan was to finish it ourselves.

Robert was thrilled to be in a different office, getting to know other members in a new detachment and having fun roaring up and down the freeway, writing tickets like he had never done before. The traffic was very heavy here compared to the little town of Vanderhoof. He was happy to go to work and life was exciting in this part of the world. The highways were very busy as everyone heading into Vancouver or coming out of Vancouver had to drive through Hope.

Hope was called the "Gateway to Holiday Land" but we called it the town of extremes! We moved into our house the first weekend of July and it was so hot we could barely survive. We did not have air conditioning in the house when we bought it, but this didn't last too long. After unpacking one or two boxes we would be so hot we would have to sit down to cool off! After a week of 40 degrees Celsius, Robert had an air conditioner installed. We hadn't realized that Hope would be so hot – we had heard from so many people that it mostly just rained there!

One day turned into the next and the summer just flew by. I was really enjoying being out of Vanderhoof and not having to worry about Robert giving out tickets to people I knew. He was so busy at work and spending so much time there that Cindy and I were on our own a lot. I was lonely, since I didn't know anyone, so Cindy and I spent hours wandering the malls and shopping in Chilliwack, just 30 minutes away. Hope wasn't really so bad after all – a 30-minute drive was quite enjoyable and the scenery was very beautiful. We also spent a lot of time at Kawkawa Lake watching the geese, or out in the front yard running through the sprinklers, or cooling off in her little pool. We weren't used to this hot, humid weather but we were enjoying the life.

One morning while we were out in the front yard, a neighbour lady came over to me and introduced herself. She then quickly asked me, "Are you the Nanny? We never see the wife around so we were wondering if this cop was married."

I didn't quite know if this was a good thing or a bad thing. I did look very young, but calmly explained that I was not the Nanny and that I was the wife! It was quite shocking to her but we soon had a laugh about it and it was the beginning of a great neighbourly friendship.

Garage Work Never Ends - More Month Than Money

As the summer ended and tourists started dissipating, life would get back to normal in the little town of Hope. The population went from around 4000 during the school year to about 15,000 every day in the summer months. The restaurants and hotels had to make their money during the peak season, so we hadn't experienced what Hope was really like yet. September was another beautiful month and Robert was enjoying the new office and his work environment. He had a great partner and he looked forward to going to work each day. He always had stories to share when he got home, some good, some not so good, some scary, some not so scary, stopping this celebrity or that judge, or this Hell's Angel etc. etc. Some things he wouldn't tell me and I was probably better off not knowing. His stories were interesting and exciting, but I really didn't worry too much about him racing up and down the freeway at 200 kilometers an hour to give someone a speeding ticket – how ironic – with me left at home with a small child to look after. People always asked me if I worried about him on the road so much, but I could honestly say that I tried not to think about it because I had given this to my Maker long ago. I firmly believed and still believe that when it is our time to go we will go, regardless of what we are doing.

Things were somewhat tight financially as there was a freeze on pay raises in the federal government for 7 years. We contemplated whether I should go back to work part-time at the bank in Hope, so I applied and was accepted for casual work at the CIBC in town. I had become good friends with another member's wife in town who had children and she offered to babysit for me when I was working. This arrangement was really good and gave me a chance to get out and meet some other people, as well as make a bit of extra cash for me and the sitter.

Robert was not only a cop but also a certified auto-mechanic and he enjoyed working in the garage on his days off. He not only loved to fix up old cars, he also restored them from the ground up. He was soon known around town for doing odd jobs in the shop, so he was never for lack of garage work. This extra money would help feed his habit for restoring old cars. His favourite car was a 69 Chevelle which was very hard to find, but he found a 70 Chevelle that would do the trick! It was a good stress reliever from work and a good distraction for him when he was on graveyard shifts. Now he had work and play and a family to look after and life was fairly good. Since the pay in the RCMP wasn't really that great we often wondered how we paid our bills and managed from month to month, but with a little help from garage work and the little extra I made we seemed to get by okay. We weren't eating steak for dinner but we certainly were not starving and we could still go out for a coffee now and then. What more could we ask for?

The Ultimatum

I enjoyed being a mom and it wasn't long before I quit my casual job at the bank, as I was just too sick and tired to be dragging myself off to work. The 9-month flu was hitting me again and in the next summer, late in August, our second baby girl, Kayce Lynn, arrived safe and sound. We were so blessed to have another beautiful daughter and I was excited for each of them to have a sister, as I never had one. I had struggled again throughout my pregnancy but Robert was very good at stepping in to help whenever he was needed. My parents loved to come and visit and they were so helpful when I was in hospital with Kayce. Bob continued to work and visit us in hospital while Cindy enjoyed spending quality time with Grandma and Papa. When Kayce was just 5 days old, with the help of grandparents, we all headed down to Expo 86 in Vancouver, and our sweet baby girl was as good as gold. Being so close to the big city did have its perks. Maybe Hope wasn't so bad after all.

We were fortunate enough to have a perfectly healthy baby girl this time. It was so much easier to have a newborn in the house the second time around and we were relieved that she had a healthy heart! Cindy was growing and was such a joy to have around, but she had a lot of ear infections which also took a lot of extra love and patience to deal with. Not only were we seeing cardiologists but also ear, nose and throat doctors, and getting very little sleep! Cindy ended up with tubes in her ears seven times, starting when she was 11 months old and almost every year thereafter until she was 9 years old, as well as having to have her adenoids and tonsils out. She had so many ear infections and sore throats as a small child but, despite all the pain she experienced, she was really quite a content, happy child.

Kayce was a very content, happy baby until she started suffering from stomach problems. This seemed to get worse as she got older and when she was about a year and a half, she was eventually hospitalized for a few nights and they put her on a clear fluid diet that was strictly apple juice, water or Jell-O. This ended up settling her stomach, but unfortunately got her addicted to apple juice which became a battle for quite some time. She would come to me for weeks and just beg for sips of apple juice to which I would have to refuse. We literally had to wean her off juice as though it was a very addictive drug.

Graveyard shifts were especially hard on us as a family. I would try and get up as soon as I heard a child crying, but as sleep deprivation became the norm, our fuses were getting shorter. Robert would struggle to get himself out the door to work after a sleepless night, and I would long to just go to work for a rest from sick kids. I wondered how we would survive. One lady always seemed to remind me that "this too would pass." Kayce and Cindy did outgrow these childhood illnesses but it did take its toll on us at the time.

Our two little girls became the best of friends and it was a pleasure to have them in our lives. We met new people in our community and in our church and soon we had close friends who became like family to us. When you have no family around for support your friends become your family and you help each other survive the ups and downs of life. We were so lucky to find friends like this so soon after moving to Hope. I had girlfriends, our girls had friends and Robert had work, friends and his garage!

His hobby of fixing and tinkering on cars was getting a little more extended week after week. The more he did, the more he wanted to do, and of course the money was feeding his Chevelle habit, so he always needed to do just a little bit more. As I was home with 2 little children and not working outside of the house, I wanted him to spend a bit more time with us and give me a bit of a reprieve from the house, sleepless nights, and sick kids. He, on the other hand, saw his days off as time to make some extra money and ended up spending a lot of time in the garage. This was great down time for him and he did need the stress relief from work. He was also sleep deprived and so many days he would just enjoy pushing the lawnmower around the yard, not having to deal with people or anything urgent. Time would always seem to slip away from him; 10 minutes would be an hour, 1 hour would turn into 3 hours and he just lost all sense of time when he was in this head space. The days would be gone if I didn't remind him to come in and eat, or to come in and spend time with our girls, or to spend time with me. "Just a few more minutes," he would say, and soon we were arguing about those few extra minutes that turned into hours.

After months of seeming like a single parent, my patience was running very thin. Yes, I had friends and was coping, but I didn't just want to cope. I wanted a relationship with the cop I married. Yes, he had a stressful job and yes he needed a stress reliever and yes I needed to be more patient, but I had given up my own career to marry this man and I wanted some time with him. I had moved away from my family and friends to be a stay-at-home mom, so I felt that he needed to compromise and pay some attention to his wife and children, and stop using the need for extra cash as an excuse. If he thought the Chevelle was going to come in the way of his wife and children, then he had another thing coming. I was not about to compromise our marriage and children just to feed his addiction to cars. He had lived this way for his bachelor years but his priorities needed revising.

I arranged for a sitter and we ended up going out for coffee one day because I told him we needed to talk about a few things without the kids. He knew that I wasn't happy with how much time he was spending in the garage, but he was not prepared for what he was about to hear. We had quite a major discussion that day on his obsession with the Chevelle and I ended up giving him an ultimatum.

It was either going to be the kids and I or the Chevelle, but I was no longer willing to let him put his car before his family; the girls needed him and so did I. His priorities needed adjusting and it was time to make it happen. This was not easy to say nor was it easy to hear, but this would keep our marriage together.

A few days later we were heading into town for another coffee date, when suddenly Robert blurted out to me that he had listed his car – the Chevelle – in the Buy and Sell magazine. I couldn't believe what I had just heard! I thought he was crazy as this was his prize possession. He had spent so much time and effort getting it up and running and looking real pretty and now he was selling it? He had hardly enjoyed driving it yet! I hadn't meant for him to let it go, just to spend a bit more time with his girls. We had a good discussion about his car over coffee, but he was adamant that it was time to sell it and move on to a new project. The fun and stress relief for him was in the actual work of the project; he was ready to adjust his priorities and find a new project where it didn't matter how long it took to get it on the road. I was quite stunned to say the least, but when the buyer drove it out of our driveway a few weeks later, we were both a bit teary and sad. It was a beautiful looking car that made peoples' heads turn.

Flipping Houses to Get Ahead – Are We Crazy?

Time to re-focus; it wasn't long before we found another way to make a bit of cash. Our goal was to get rid of our mortgage somehow. We knew the market had been way down when we bought in 85 but also knew the market was going up now, just a few years later. We had been slowly working on getting our basement finished (Bob was a jack of all trades) and now we could list the house. We ended up meeting with a realtor in town who thought we could make some money on our house, and she helped us find another house that would work for our family. She also felt that this house would sell when the time came for us to have to move with the RCMP. We decided to go ahead with this plan much to the dismay of almost everyone we knew. They all thought we were absolutely crazy! Why would we sell our nice house that was just finished the way we liked it, to move into a smaller house that needed a whole pile more work! Even though we were going against advice, we clung to our dreams and went ahead and trusted our realtor. We listed the house and started decluttering.

Garage sales were the fad at that time so we decided to try one for ourselves. My Mom loved to put on garage sales, so she came over and spent a week with me and helped us out. We had a great time trying to sell all our "junk" (one man's junk is another man's treasure), so we didn't have to move it when the time came. Our treasures sailed out the door and we had so much fun that day making memories that are still in our minds today. My Mom had the reputation of being able to sell a fridge to an Eskimo, and we still laugh about her selling a suit jacket to a man who needed a jacket for a wedding, even though he couldn't do up the buttons.

"The style is to leave the jacket open anyways," said my Mom. "No one will know that you can't do it up." He ended up buying the jacket and went away proud as punch that he had found a jacket for the wedding. We had such a good laugh over that scene for many, many years to come and I am smiling even now as I write about this memory.

Not only did we sell the suit jacket that day but we ended up finding a buyer for our house, so it was a very profitable garage sale.

A month later we were moving into a smaller house near the railroad tracks. This house needed landscaping done amongst other smaller repairs and just some tender loving care. It took some time getting used to the new area, but we were happy there and we were very happy with the chunk of cash we could put down on the mortgage. Now it was time to landscape and work on this property so that we could find a buyer and move again. Hopefully one or two more moves and we would be free and clear of the mortgage, if we played our cards right. Maybe we were crazy but at least we were crazy together.

Hawaiian Vacation

Staying married is not as easy as it seems; marriage is like a partnership and both partners have to do their share. I think people who say marriage is a breeze are fooling themselves. It takes compromising and hard work to make it through things you don't agree on. Both partners have to give in sometimes and do things the other person's way, and this can be difficult if you really don't agree with the strategy. One of our slogans was that if you always agreed with each other, then someone was being the underdog because usually two people have some differing opinions and you don't always agree. That is what makes a marriage unique, two people becoming one. Sometimes we would agree but other times we had totally different opinions on the way we wanted to handle situations. Usually after a time of discussion, we might not agree, but we would have decided which direction we were taking together.

Most marriages go through good times, hard times, happy times and sad times but I wanted us to have more happy times than hard times. I wanted our children to have fond memories of their childhood and so I was always trying to come up with new adventures we could do together as a family and that would create happy memories. Sometimes in my endeavour to make this happen, the bottom would fall out of my plan because one person wouldn't be on board, but other times my efforts paid off. Our marriage had its ups and downs like most couples, but we were both determined to work things out. We had already seen so many divorces and separations within the RCMP that we were extra determined to make it work. My life with a cop was for the long term, not the short term. We had lots of struggles throughout the years with sick children, not enough sleep, not enough sex, not enough time together, not enough money, working through different cultures, having different values and goals but nothing really different from what other couples were also experiencing. We felt we had done fairly well in our first few years of marriage, having come from different backgrounds and having to work through the trials of sick children and the lack of sleep. We were given so much free advice and when you have tried all the free advice you finally come to the realization that you just have to figure it out on your own, because no two children are alike! We had moved away from family and had to rely on each other and this caused us to work harder at our relationship.

We decided that we would try camping together because this was one way of having a holiday without having to spend too much money. We found a small hard-walled tent trailer we could afford when we first moved to Hope and ended up discovering a campsite that we absolutely loved in Oliver, BC, on Tuc el Nuit Lake. We started camping with our girls when they were quite young and ended up going to this campsite as a family for 15 years. We went every summer, first for one week each summer and then for two, because we loved it there so much. We could actually relax there and didn't have to make too many decisions. We didn't have to worry about the kids as this was a very friendly, family campground. We could lie on the beach, make castles in the sand or swim and spend hours in the water. We looked forward to this holiday time in Oliver year after year and we made so many good memories in this place.

We had never been away from our children to go on a big vacation, like some of our friends had, and we felt that our marriage would benefit from a holiday away together. My parents came to the rescue once again. Our girls just loved to be with their grandparents and so we felt that they were old enough and sleeping well enough now that we could actually leave them long enough for us to take a trip to Hawaii. We hadn't been anywhere out of the country together and we really looked forward to getting away and enjoying some heat in the middle of winter. We scraped enough money together and booked a 10-day trip to Hawaii at the end of February. We went with another couple and shared the cost of the condo so it was quite doable for us. Before we knew it we were enjoying the beaches in Maui. How fabulous it was. We thoroughly enjoyed the time we had together, swam and snorkeled in the ocean, relaxed in the sun, sat in the hot tub, ate out in fancy restaurants in the evening, and relished our time together again as a couple, which rejuvenated our relationship once again.

While away we had time to reflect on our goals and the purpose for our lives. We were accountable to each other and kept each other motivated to reach these goals. We would set financial goals, short term and long term, and strive hard to attain them. We usually were able to reach most of our targets but sometimes we had to readjust them midway.

A Third Child

We had always wished to have four children but the two difficult pregnancies I had and the sleepless nights we experienced for so many years made us really question whether we should have more children or not. Cindy was 6 and Kayce was 4 and life was starting to get easier as they were older and sleeping better. We decided that four children were still what we wanted and it wasn't long before we were expecting our third child. We were excited now about having made this decision. The house that we had moved into was smaller than the previous one and so adding another child to this smaller house was going to take some adjusting. It was time to start thinking about selling and moving again.

This pregnancy was worse for me than the last two and instead of being able to help out more, I was mostly bedridden for the first few months of the pregnancy. My husband had to pick up the slack even more this time, and we were so fortunate to have two girls who played well together and who were old enough to help out quite a bit. They weren't babies anymore, so they could play for an hour or two while I was resting and I didn't have to worry that they were getting into trouble. I was so weak I could barely get out of bed some days, and on those days Robert would have to go to work, come home and feed the girls lunch, go back to work, come home from work, make dinner and put the girls to bed, while I just laid in bed or on the couch all day. Sounds pathetic I know, but that's all I could muster up. Robert was a trooper and he knew how to clean and cook and get things done.

About the 4th month into my pregnancy, some friends of ours were coming through Hope and asked if we could meet them in town for a visit. It was my first time out of the house in weeks and I thought the outing might do me some good, but half an hour into the visit I needed to go home and get back into bed; I was just too weak to sit up and visit. Some people glow through pregnancy but certainly not me! I had some other complications as well as feeling weak and anemic. I had a condition called cholestasis which was characterized by severe generalized itching. I ended up seeing a specialist in Chilliwack who gave me his home phone number and I was told to call him if I started thinking suicide. This itching was unbearable at times and I would be up wandering the house at night, crying for an end to this horrible feeling. Only people who have also experienced this seem to relate to this sense of not being able to cope. The doctor did say that if and when I couldn't cope any longer, he would induce me, although the longer I could hold off, the safer for the baby. This condition usually goes away soon after the child is born and since I had already had it with my first pregnancy, I knew that each day closer to the due date was giving my child a little better start in life.

One cold winter night in late November I woke up with contractions. It was going to be another long day, but soon my itching would be over. I stayed in bed and Robert got up to take our girls to Sunday School, where we had arranged for our good friends to pick them up and take them home for the day while Robert would attend to me. The power went off for hours that day and we spent most of the day under the covers to keep warm, as this was one of the coldest winter days we had that year. By 6 o'clock that evening Robert practically had to carry me into the hospital because I couldn't walk, and by 8 p.m. we had a healthy baby boy, Colin Robert. We were excited to have two girls and now a boy and I knew that this was going to be our last. I just couldn't handle the thought of going through another 9 months like that again. It was hard on all of us so three children would make our family just perfect.

A Cold Christmas

Everyone told us that the third child was always the easy child. I was sure longing for them to be right, but in the quietness of my heart I knew they were probably wrong. We seemingly were destined to have babies that slept poorly but people also told us that if we had children who were challenging as babies, generally the teenage years were easier to handle, so we clung to this hope.

Christmas this year, 1990, was an unusually cold winter. We headed up to my parents' house for Christmas with a 3-week old baby and looked forward to this special time together with them. It was so nice to have extra help from my mom with three little children and the girls just loved to be at Grandma and Papa's house. I treasured the visits with my mom and all the help I received with a new baby and she doted on us and made us feel so welcome. Our little boy had gotten more colicky as the weeks went by, so being able to rest when he slept knowing that my mom was caring for the girls was such a gift. She loved the Christmas season and we cherished this time in her cozy decorated home. The five of us slept in the "dungeon" as we called it, and it was so exciting for the girls to sleep at Grandma's house and feel the excitement of Christmas in the air. We baked cookies and buns and had tea parties with the girls. We went shopping and went out for treats and visited with family and friends. We ended up having to stay an extra week this particular visit as the temperature went to below minus 50 degrees Fahrenheit. We just couldn't take a chance on heading out with a baby in that kind of weather, so luckily the Christmas gift of a Nintendo game really came in handy that year. After two straight weeks of these freezing temperatures we were all beginning to feel just a little too closed in. Robert was getting antsy so on the first morning that it went up to minus 35, we packed up and headed out. Bob needed to get back to work but it was still a bit foolish to travel in this cold temperature. He was adamant, how cops can be, but we prayed for protection as we headed back up the Vanderhoof hill out of town with three little children. About 2 to 3 hours from Vanderhoof the weather started warming up and we weren't quite so anxious about travelling the rest of the way home. We were taking quite the risk driving in those weather conditions. If we did break down or have any trouble at all, no one would survive for very long in those freezing temperatures. We made it home safe and sound once again and life resumed its normal routine, but not for too long!

Moving Time Again

We decided our little house wasn't really big enough for the five of us so we began the search for a new house. We spoke with our realtor once again and she thought we could make some money on this place now, as the market was still going up and we were at the right place at the right time. We thought it might be nice to try building a house this time, as our good friend was a contractor in Hope. We found a piece of property in town on 5th Avenue, close to the Elementary School. It would be so nice for the girls to come home for lunches if they so desired and give them a quick reprieve from school. We looked at many different house plans and found one we both liked, that we could afford, and would fit our family of five. It was a mild winter this year in Hope, unlike the ghastly freezing temperatures of Vanderhoof, so it wasn't long before plans were well on their way and we were building our very own custom house. It went up fast and by the end of April we were moving again. This time people didn't think we were quite so crazy, because it actually made sense to move into a bigger house rather than the one we were living in. The truth was though, that this had all been in our plan to pay off our mortgage and get ahead financially. Yes, it was work, but we were not scared of work, and we bonded in another way through meeting these goals. It took effort on both of our parts and hard work from both of us to meet these deadlines and goals with three little children. We were proud of ourselves and celebrated our victory; to be mortgage free by the age of 35 was quite an accomplishment. It was part of our financial goal planning and we have benefitted from that ever since.

In the spring we decided that we needed to start exercising together. We didn't really have money to go to the gym, but I loved to walk and Robert needed to walk to help relieve some stress, so walking would kill two birds with one stone. We would actually be able to have adult conversations together while we walked and we would both benefit from the stress relief of getting daily exercise. As we struggled to make this a habit, we found how it helped us communicate more and more. We found a loop that we would walk that took us about an hour and during our walks we had time to work through issues that we were dealing with. The more we walked and talked, the more we looked forward to these walks together and our sharing time. It was a habit that we strived to keep throughout his career as a cop.

A Sick Boy

About a year after moving into our new house, we decided we would try to have another weekend away from children. We were celebrating our 10th wedding anniversary and so a weekend away sounded delightful. We made arrangements for us to go to a marriage retreat that we heard was supposed to help make a marriage stronger. We felt any input into our marriage was a good thing, as members all around us were getting divorced right before our eyes. We were determined to make our marriage work so we thought putting some work into our marriage might be a great idea.

We left for the weekend, and had a wonderful time away, only to come home to a very sick boy. He had a fever of over 104F. so we rushed him to the Emergency that very night. Robert thought he had scarlet fever and, if so, he would need to go on antibiotics immediately. The doctor in Emerg that night looked at our sick little boy and said that he just had a reaction to something and that we should give him Benadryl and take him home. Robert argued and persisted that he had scarlet fever, but the doctor didn't agree and sent us off with some Benadryl for the night. We both didn't sleep a wink that night as our poor little guy just got worse and worse throughout the night. The following morning we phoned up our own GP and got in to see him first thing. As he took a look at Colin the first words out of his mouth were "This kid has scarlet fever!" You can imagine the outrage from us and from our doctor after hearing about our Emerg visit the previous night, but we had to move forward now and get him on some antibiotics to fight off the infection.

We went home and three days later we were off to the doctor's office again. Colin would need to have some regular checkups for the year to come due to the way scarlet fever can affect the heart, but this visit was not about his scarlet fever. Colin had developed a hernia that sent us down to Children's Hospital for an emergency surgery; this hernia could become strangulated at any moment which would be life threatening if not dealt with. The doctor told me to call Robert at work and we were to leave immediately and head into the emergency department at Children's Hospital. Our doctor phoned the hospital and prepared them for our visit and the need for surgery. The following morning Colin was undergoing hernia surgery, and soon after he woke up we were on the road home again. This was a total whirlwind of a trip for us and exhaustion was setting in again. He was still recovering from scarlet fever and was still on antibiotics so for now he should be okay for the next few days. We might not be okay, but he would be.

Life went back to normal for a few months, until summertime, when we had another hospital experience. Colin was now two years old and he loved to be out playing with his sisters. We were in the kitchen having a cup of coffee with my parents when suddenly we heard this bloodcurdling scream. You just know in your heart when it's really bad, and this was one of those times. Robert rushed out the door to the back yard and in a minute he yelled at us that we had to rush to the hospital. All his first aid knowledge went out the window when it came to this accident. He shouldn't have lifted Colin, but instinct as a parent is different than being on the job as a first responder.

"Grab a pillow" he yelled, "you drive while I hold him. He has a broken leg." He positioned Colin on the pillow so that he didn't have to move him too much and off we were to Emerg.

The kids had been playing on the trampoline, not actually jumping on it I must add, and Colin fell off of it onto the grass. No one saw how he landed but Robert knew that it was bad. The doctor tried to get the IV into his poor little hand but after multiple attempts without success we were ready to punch him out and call someone else. The nurses wouldn't even try and this doc just couldn't find his vein. Another doctor finally came in the room and before you could count to three she had it done. Hearing your child screaming from pain is just too much for a mother to bear, and we both could hardly take much more of it. X-rays were done revealing a spiral femur break from hip to knee and soon we were in the ambulance on our way to Children's Hospital once again, only this time it would be for a whole lot longer. The next couple of weeks were like a nightmare from hell and recalling the events is still hard for me and brings up depressing memories.

We had been planning our camping vacation to Oliver, where we loved to go and which was just five days away. Now our whole vacation was spent at Children's Hospital trying to get through one hour at a time. Plans can change in an instant, reminding us that we are not really in control, but it is God who plans our days.

Colin was put on morphine for the next couple of days and was in an inverted position with his head down and feet up in traction for the next 2 weeks. He had weights hanging from his feet to pull the bone back in alignment. Then he would be in a hip spica cast for the next couple of months which pretty much made us house bound for the foreseeing future.

The 2-week hospital experience was not any fun at all, but we survived it and came out of hospital a lot better off than many other children do. When you think your situation is bad, you just need to take a look around you in a hospital and see that there are always other people way worse off than yourself. Doing this helped give us a positive perspective on our own situation, and yet our experience was not a happy one either. It was so hard to watch our little 2-year-old suffer like he did with the pain of the break, not being able to eat properly lying in this inverted position, nor being able to sit up or roll over or even just to move his leg because of it being in traction. Then there were other issues to deal with as well, like bathroom issues, which became huge with gravity working against him. Trying to get through each day seemed like forever but eventually, after 14 days in traction, the doctors were happy with the alignment of the femur. They put him under anesthesia at this point to take the bandages and weights off his legs and then put him into a hip spica cast. He picked a red colour for his cast and this cast went from his chest down his trunk and then down the whole right leg. When Robert lifted him up to hold him after he was out of recovery, Colin couldn't even hold his head up after being inverted for so long. The doctors told us that he would be set back socially about a year, but that he would catch up again in a few years. This was because he went from being totally independent at 2 years of age to becoming totally dependent again, and this setback takes a few years to regain self-confidence. We hoped that this would be our last hospital experience for a long, long time.

My parents were there again to support us through this time and looked after the girls while Bob and I spent 2 weeks with Colin in the hospital. We were so lucky, Robert and I, because without the help from my parents I don't know how we would have coped. The following months were hard and I wouldn't wish that on anyone, but we made it through leaning on each other and with the help from my folks.

How to Survive the Ride?

Walking was a very necessary component for me to survive the ride with my cop. Not only did it give us time to visit and the daily exercise that we needed, we also worked through many issues during our hours of walking and talking. We laughed, dreamed and set goals while de-stressing and freeing our minds of clutter. We walked and talked, laughed and cried, shared and prayed and managed to get through the tough times by communicating even when we didn't feel like it. Making a habit of walking and talking is another step in surviving the ride.

Chapter 4
Hard Good-Byes, from Lush to Desert!

Hardship for Our Children

We started to get antsy about moving. Moving was beginning to get into our veins and we seemed to enjoy the thrill of what was around the next corner. Robert was tired of racing up and down the freeway in his hot little police mustang. He was tired of writing 50 tickets a day and busting his butt for no raise in 7 years. When would the federal government start to pay their police force employees the same as other police organizations in Canada? We could have jumped ship and stayed in one place with a provincial police force, but Robert was a Mountie through and through. He loved his job, for the most part, and his goal was always to finish well and to stay in the RCMP until he received his 35-year pin. It was quite the goal but it was his personal life long goal and I wanted to help him achieve it. I had given up my career and pensionable job so we felt we needed to get as much as we could out of his. This was one of our long term goals, the question was – would he actually make 35 years?

We had been in Hope for 10 years now and Robert knew it was time for a change. We had heard rumblings about us being transferred, so it was better for us to ask than wait for a transfer out of the blue. We got the call sometime in the spring and didn't know where it would lead us. We were really wishing for Kamloops, as there was a private school where we were hoping our children could attend. We couldn't really afford private schooling but all three children would be in school soon and I could go back to work, which would help us financially. I had already started serving part-time in a little restaurant on Robert's days off and I was enjoying getting out and having some adult conversation. Once all three kids were in school then maybe I could focus on my own career again. I loved to get out and meet new people and the change in atmosphere was good for me. Being a stay-at-home mom while the children were little was wonderful, but once I could help out financially it would take some of the pressure off of Robert.

On the transfer form Robert put down he wanted Kamloops, Kamloops or Kamloops! We were told that there was no chance of us ever getting to Kamloops. Everyone wanted to go there! However, due to very unfortunate circumstances, we somehow found ourselves transferred to Kamloops. There had been a terrible accident involving a police officer, suddenly an opening came available and the position was given to us. We were thankful for the posting, just not under these circumstances. We also knew that this move would be hard on the girls.

We had put down a lot of roots in Hope over the last 10 years. Two of our three children were born there, so it felt like home to all of us. Cindy, our oldest daughter was now 11, Kayce was 9, and Colin was 4. The place I was 'never moving to' had become our home. Strangely enough, we were still excited to be moving to a new location for another adventure.

We have good and bad memories from Hope. Robert mostly enjoyed his time at this detachment, although some incidents he will never forget. I recall a time when he was called to a bad accident up the Coquihala highway. This was a fatality that involved a family bringing their daughter to university. No fatalities are good, but some are worse than others and this one really stands out in his memory. Some scenes play over and over in his mind and this one still haunts him to this day. He was home late for supper that night and he hadn't eaten all day so he was hungry. Our family loved home-made macaroni and cheese and I had made that for supper this particular night. He walked into the kitchen for something to eat and saw the dish of macaroni and cheese, then turned around quickly and left the room without saying a word. He didn't want to upset the kids but he just couldn't stomach eating it that night, as it reminded him so much of the remains at the accident scene. He couldn't eat macaroni and cheese for a long time after this, and he still would prefer not to have it now.

All three children had experienced Children's Hospital and these were things I didn't need to remember, but as a mother you just don't forget. Cindy was there for a tonsillectomy, adenoidectomy, multiple myringotomies and multiple visits to her pediatric cardiologist for her congenital heart defect. Kayce was there for a tonsillectomy and she also had a stint in the Hope hospital for suspected intussusception, which she thankfully outgrew. Colin had two stays at Children's Hospital, first for his inguinal hernia and then for his broken femur. Two years later he wound up in the emergency department in Edmonton as well, when he fell and broke his arm on the playground. We were happy that Cindy had been cleared by her pediatric cardiologist and told that she didn't need to be seen at Children's Hospital again. Kayce and Colin were doing well, so hopefully we were finished with hospitals for a while.

We had enjoyed the outdoors near Hope, including swimming, camping, hiking, skiing, as well as trips to the water slides and to the Flintstones Park. Our children had such close friends we knew it would be very hard emotionally for them to move away. Sometimes I wondered whether a career in the RCMP was worth the emotional upset of moving and how it would affect our children in the long run.

Feelings swept to the side, we pushed onwards. Our nice new custom house was listed and it wasn't too long before the Sold sign went up. We were moving to an area where the housing market was higher and we wanted to be careful not to have to go into another mortgage. We went on a very quick house hunting trip because I had started serving in a restaurant and only had three days off. We jam-packed our days and looked at close to 50 houses in this short time frame. We finally decided on a house that we were going to buy when a member came along and told us not to buy in that area. Members tend to look out for the welfare of other members, so we felt we needed to listen to his advice and we ripped up the purchase forms and started over again. There had been one other house that we felt suited all our needs, but it was just a little out of our price range. After sleeping on the decision and looking at the house again, we decided to bite the bullet and plunge forward. This was in a better location for us and we felt good about our decision.

We had also met the next door neighbour who had offered to make dinner for us the day we moved in. It wasn't long after we moved in that we became lifelong friends and we have spent many hours throughout the years enjoying coffee together and encouraging one another.

After three days of an all-consuming house hunting trip, we were exhausted. I recall that I had to be at work the next morning by 6 a.m. to open the restaurant where I worked, and as I staggered out of bed it wasn't long before I knew I was quite ill. Had the house hunting trip really been that stressful for me? I made it in to work and started feeling very light headed and weak. I really was getting sick, so I had to call someone in to take my place. This was so unusual for me as I was hardly ever sick. We determined that I must have had food poisoning as I had never been that violently ill in such a few short hours. It wasn't long before I was soon feeling well again, but that house hunting trip has made a permanent mark in my memory.

We were moving the beginning of September, but in order for the kids to start their new school on the first day, we had to go on ahead to Kamloops without Robert. We were going to be in a motel for a few nights while the moving company packed up our house and brought our things to Kamloops. I hated good-byes and we were only moving about 2 hours away, so we decided we wouldn't say good-bye but that we would just say "see you soon." We would try and make the good-bye as easy as we could and yet that was a complete failure. You can't take emotion out of the picture, it just doesn't work. The girls were leaving their best friends and saying good-bye was such a hard thing for me to watch. I could live with the grieving for myself, but not for my children. By the time we merged onto the freeway heading to Kamloops we cranked up the music and the four of us all cried our eyes out for the next hour. Once our tears were shed and there were no more left to fall, we began to be thankful and tried to put things into perspective. We were only 2 hours away and we could certainly visit our friends, but this was so much darn harder than I thought it was going to be.

Hope was so lush and green, with so many beautiful azaleas and wild rhododendrons, that driving into Kamloops with the tumbleweeds blowing over the roads and looking up into the brown desert hills made me long for the mountains of Hope already.

Hardship on Parents

September was a busy month trying to settle into a new city, learning where to drive, which stores to shop at, where to buy groceries, a whole new life. Robert was making his way in the new detachment and learning the ropes around the office, as well as all the highways he had to patrol. The girls started at their new school which we hoped would be a wonderful experience for them with likeminded children. Our daughters were keen to learn and excel at their education. Kayce was quick to make new friends and soon had a bunch of girls to hang out with. But the older girls were quite cliquish and Cindy, at the age of 11, found it a bit more difficult making friends. Grade 7 can be a hard year for most kids as they are blossoming into adults, but Cindy was a very determined person who seemed to know her purpose and what she wanted to do with her life. She had a real love of art early in her childhood and we sought to develop this gift by giving her art lessons from quite a young age. Now in the quietness of her loneliness she began to delve into her art hobby more and more. Kayce, on the other hand, seemed to be doing very well at school but would come home and cry herself to sleep night after night for months and was inconsolable at times. These few months were agonizing for me as I questioned in my heart whether the opportunities we sought after were worth making our children so dreadfully unhappy. The question of why we do what we do and what our life purpose is were at the forefront of my mind.

Colin was only 4 years of age when we moved to Kamloops and, because of his set-back when he was 2, was still a shy, quiet boy and wasn't really ready for the social aspect of school. The move wasn't so hard on him but, after talking with many teachers and doing a lot of research, we decided to homeschool him for the fall and try sending him to school in January. Academically he was ready for school, but he had been set back with his independence just like the doctor had said he would be. In January we decided to send him to the private school and see how he managed. He needed friends too, and we hoped this first year of kindergarten would bring him out of his shell. As the months went by, the good-byes in the morning were getting harder rather than easier and my heart couldn't take a whole lot more of him feeling so forsaken. I knew that I would not do another year like this one, either we needed to homeschool him or find a school in our neighbourhood where he was close to home.

In the spring of 96, my parents came to visit and my Dad was in the process of buying a new semi-truck. He was still doing business, although he was semi-retired, and my mom decided to stay and help me out for a week and spend a bit more time with us. About 2 days later, Mom and I had gone over to my aunt's house for a visit while the kids were in school. While we were there we got a phone call that no one ever wants to get. Suddenly life changed for my parents in the blink of an eye. My dad had just had a major stroke and the doctors didn't expect him to make it through the night!

There was only one flight a day out of Kamloops to Prince George at this time. We phoned and explained our situation and they actually held the plane for Mom so that she could make it home that evening to see my dad. He survived the night, to the surprise of the doctors, but his prognosis was very bleak. Early the next morning, Robert and I packed up our family and headed to Prince George not knowing what to expect. Dad surprised everyone, and although the road was going to be long and grim ahead for him, he made it through this stroke and recovered over the next few years to the point where he could function without too much extra care. My mother had to give up her career as an LPN to care for Dad, but she was prepared to do so and did it without any regret. Seeing your parents in this kind of state is dreadfully painful and so the months and years following were hard for us all. The dad I knew had changed and my mom now had a full time job looking after her husband. Papa had changed and so life for the grandkids had changed as well. We kept reminding ourselves that the only thing constant in life was change and that we had to accept this and move on, regardless of whether we liked it or not. People say that difficult circumstances either make your marriage stronger or break you apart. I guess in hindsight we clung to each other more, prayed more and realized how short life really was. We wanted to try and make the most out of every opportunity we were given, because life can change so quickly.

Changing Schools

The first year in Kamloops was difficult to say the least, but we got through it and moved forward. We decided that it was okay to change how we felt about private education. After all, how could we know if we didn't try? We tried it and all three of our children had a very tough year, so we decided it was worth the agony of starting over again. Cindy was our biggest concern as she would be starting high school all alone and this was not an easy thing to ask of her. We pondered over the right decision for a long time, but ultimately the decision was given to her. She decided that she did want to start at the public high school in the fall, as she hadn't really connected with anyone at the private school. In the end, this proved to be the right decision. She met her future husband there and she made friends easier and was much more confident in herself than the year before.

Kayce and Colin started at the elementary school in our neighbourhood. Kayce already had a friend who was changing schools with her, so this was an easy transition which proved to be the right decision. She blossomed at her new school and was a beaming light to those around her. I spoke to Colin's grade 1 teacher at the beginning of the year and explained how hard kindergarten had been for the two of us. I explained that I was giving this a trial period for one week and that if we had any days like the previous year, I would be homeschooling Colin for Grade 1. She was a grandmother type of teacher and very respectful of my decision. After the first day I could tell that being in a school that was closer to home was the right decision for him as well. This teacher gave Colin the courage to stand up for himself and he flourished throughout that year. We had wished to move to Kamloops in the hopes of giving our children the best private education, but in the end private education was not the best for our children. Our kids needed to blend into the public system and they did this very well.

Taking in a Student

I started a new job the year we moved to Kamloops as well, working part-time at a fast food store close to our house so that I could help pay for the private education. I usually worked when Robert was on days off so we didn't have to pay for a sitter, which made it somewhat worthwhile working at a minimum wage job. I loved getting out and making new friends and it was here that I met a wonderful university student, Petra-Ann, who became a very close friend for life. She was living with her aunt and uncle at the time, but a year later they moved and Petra-Ann needed a place to live to finish school. Robert and I had talked about renting a room to a university student, so we offered her a room in our basement if she wanted to live with a family and share the house with us. She accepted our offer and soon our house was buzzing with energy and excitement. Our kids were so excited to have a new friend in the house and it wasn't long before they bonded and Petra-Ann became more like a sister to them than a renter. This was a blessing in so many ways. They were no longer so lonely and were beginning to enjoy life and be happy once again. What a comforting thing for a parent to see their children happy and full of life. Petra-Ann was just what all of us needed at that time and the days were always sunny and bright with her in our lives.

After a year of working in the fast food service industry, I was given the opportunity to go and work for a company that printed lottery tickets. I had been hired to do reception work and a bit of accounts receivables. I was very fortunate to land a job like this, as I had no experience in reception and they were willing to train me. This job was what really got me back into the workplace and I continued to expand my skills from that time on. From there I had the courage to apply to the School District in Kamloops to work with special needs students. I had always wanted to be a teacher, but somehow this career wasn't meant to be. After being home for 12 years I didn't really think it was worth it for me to spend so much time, money and effort to go back to university to become a teacher. We talked about the pros and cons a lot, many people do pursue a career after their children are in school, but I couldn't see myself losing all that time away from my family having to study and spend so much time doing homework. I settled on becoming a teacher assistant which I did for our remaining years in Kamloops. I learned a lot and value the time I had with the School District as a support worker. I went on to study and learn sign language and was able to use these skills in working with students who required sign language. The memories of learning sign language with a wonderful colleague of mine are times that I recall with great fondness.

Learning to Let Go – the Teenage Years

The following years felt like a walk in the park. We had some bumps along the way, but nothing major to speak of compared to my dad's stroke. That kind of experience put things into perspective for us all. Colin had to have another minor little surgery, but generally we were all faring well. Robert was enjoying Kamloops and still working on muscle cars. While still in Hope he had purchased an old firebird that was completely in pieces and he was now having more time to work in the garage because we didn't have small children any more. It was a 1967 Firebird and he couldn't wait to insure it and actually enjoy driving it. He had met some other car fanatics who were like minded and so he was in his glory. I was enjoying my job too and we all felt quite settled in Kamloops, in school, with friends and in our church.

Cindy started dating which was a new challenge before us. She was only in grade 10, much too young to get so serious. I had also started dating young so this was no surprise to me, but being a cop, Robert was a little too overzealous to protect his darling girls. I had to step in many times to defend or state my case for the kids, as he often could only see the bad things that might happen if they went out or did certain things. I didn't blame him, after all, he was seeing a lot of unnatural events that carried forward into how he viewed the outside world. He was just trying to protect his children from these horrific incidents and yet sometimes this made him too overprotective. It was hard for Bob to let our children walk to school, for instance, because someone might offer to pick them up and give them a ride, but were they good drivers? There were a lot of idiots on the road! He didn't want them walking on the trails alone because they could be attacked by bears. To his defense, there were quite a few bears in the area at certain times of the year so he had good reason some days. Parties were also not a good scene on his radar, as most ended up with the police attending for mischief related calls later on into the evenings.

Robert was overprotective at times but he usually had good reason for being this way. One accident scene that he was called to just outside of Kamloops near the town of Chase was one of those scenes that affected him for the rest of his life and still bothers him to this day. This was another horrible fatality involving a mother, grandmother and two little kids in car seats. The mother was driving up a hill, called Jade Mountain, behind a semi-truck and misjudged how slow the truck was going. She pulled out to pass so as not to run into the back of the truck, but overcorrected when she saw another semi coming towards her, then hit the semi head on. Robert got to the scene, looked under the tarp in the back seat and saw two beautiful kids strapped in car seats. They looked like they were fast asleep, only they were not asleep but rather they were gone. That image still haunts him at times and deeply bothered him for a very long time. He could see his own kids in those car seats and it was no wonder why he worried about our kids riding with inexperienced drivers to and from school.

We had to learn to let go a little bit more each year, and the oldest child in a family usually has the hardest time with their parents letting go. By the time we got to the second child, we knew a little more of what to expect and so the same issues didn't seem quite so terrifying. High school, dating, working outside the home, boyfriends, drinking and driving, the list is quite extensive, but we learned to let go a little bit at a time.

Our First One Gone

We were the proud parents of an honors graduate from high school in 2001. Cindy had done very well for herself throughout high school, so the decision she had made to start at the public school 5 years previously had been the right one. She was persuaded to attend the university in Kamloops for her freshman year so that she could live at home and save money, even though this wasn't as glamorous or exciting as what her boyfriend was doing; he was heading out to UBC and she was being left behind. She had determined in her mind that she was going to go the following year regardless, and there was no persuading her otherwise, debt or no debt. When she got her acceptance to UBC she was elated and we couldn't blame her for being so excited. I had left home to go away for school as well and loved the experience, so why shouldn't she? The difference from way back then up to now was that the cost of university had increased drastically; how were we going to get her through university without student loans? She was determined though, and worked two jobs each summer just to make ends meet. She was a stubborn young woman and this was paying off. She was making her dreams become reality and we were proud of her for that.

I found this stage of letting go very difficult. I could now look back and understand why my own mother found it so hard to let me go way back then. As we drove Cindy to UBC and said our good-byes I had to really talk to myself, hold back my tears and accept the change. We had raised our children to be independent and encouraged them to follow their dreams, so now we should be happy that Cindy was doing this. Emotions somehow got in the way and I wasn't prepared for how hard this would be for me.

Fortunately, I still had Kayce and Colin at home to keep me busy. Kayce was doing very well in grade 11 and Colin was now in grade 7, almost ready for high school. Kayce was working a lot, playing soccer and taking her Grade 12 piano, so she was extremely busy. Colin was playing hockey during the winter season and golfing in the summer, so driving him to practices, watching games and taxiing him to the golf courses kept us busy and helped distract me from missing Cindy so much.

Every phase of life has its challenges, disappointments and blessings. Learning to let go and give up control is part of the process in parenting. I had a long way to go and was taking one step at a time hoping that by the time we were empty nesters I would know how to cope with the change.

How to Survive the Ride?

Every chapter in our lives is a learning process. We had seen so many changes over the last 10 years, but so much happens in the short space of 5 years. You go from having a newborn to a child in kindergarten, from total dependence to independence, from a child to a teenager, and from a young adult to a man or woman out on their own. It is crazy how this happens right before your eyes and you can't control it. We try to control too much of what happens on a daily basis and this prevents us from enjoying the ride along the way. We need to let go of things that don't really matter and that we have no control over. Letting go is not an easy task with your family, your spouse, your job, or whatever is dear to your heart, but it is a necessary component to surviving the ride.

Chapter 5
A Career for Me

Promotional Exam

The moving fever was starting to hit us again. We had lived in the same house for our whole stint in Kamloops – 10 long years. I know that doesn't sound long to some people, but to us it did. We wanted to be on the move again and Robert was hoping for a promotion. He had a hard time with the promotion process in the RCMP because he was one of the last of the baby boomers to join; he wasn't able to get promoted until later in his career. He had put his family first and I was proud of him for that. The process for promotion was changing and now he had to write competency based exams. This process was disconcerting in many ways because the young cops coming in with university degrees would get higher scores than the older, uneducated cops, therefore, the younger guys with no experience in the field were getting promoted while the older, more experienced guys were being overlooked. You can imagine what this did for the rapport in the ranks. It was, quite frankly, irritating and very unfair because there was no help or study materials available for them to learn how to write these exams. After a few attempts at writing the exams and passing, but not getting in the top 5%, Robert was discouraged and ready to just stay a constable for life. I faithfully encouraged him to keep writing, as sooner or later he would get the hang of it and do well. If he didn't write then he wouldn't have a chance at all and I knew he had what it took to do it. After some years, the RCMP finally came out with a study process to help the older guys who were not getting promoted. With some help in learning how to answer these competencies properly, Robert managed to get a very good mark on his next exam! Now he could look at becoming a corporal.

Curves – The Big Decision

We were still walking almost every night, working out the kinks that came our way and I had joined a gym called "Curves." I fell in love with this work-out and started dreaming about opening up my own Curves gym. We had always wanted to have a business and throughout the years I had experimented in Mary Kay, Linens & Lace and a few other home based businesses. I was an entrepreneur at heart, which I inherited from my father, and really wanted to try getting involved in business. Curves seemed to be just my style. There were so many of these gyms going up around the province and this company was expanding into other countries very quickly. We realized that if we wanted to be a part of this franchise we would have to get on the train or be left behind. I phoned and asked about getting a franchise in Vanderhoof, which was 7 hours from Kamloops, and they told me that they would look into the possibility and get back to me in a few days. I anxiously awaited the answer and knew that we would have to be ready to put our money down immediately or bow out. A big decision was about to be made.

If we got the go ahead for the Curves gym in Vanderhoof it would mean a move on my part and other big decisions would have to be made about Robert and his work. This was also Kayce's graduation year! She was excited to finally be finishing high school. She had finished her grade 12 piano exam and was still working almost full-time hours. Kayce would be attending university after graduation so she was planning on leaving the nest anyway, but Colin was in high school and it would be hard for him to move at this age. Kayce was a pleasure to have around and it was going to be hard to see her leave the nest. At least we still had Colin and, hopefully, by the time he graduated I would have gotten the hang of the empty nest feeling.

Around supper time a few days later the phone rang. It was time to make a decision. There had already been someone who had applied for the Curves franchise in Vanderhoof, but the offer had fallen through and they were giving me the opportunity. I was only given a few days to decide as there were 4 more inquiries for Vanderhoof after me. Like I said, Curves was moving ahead and we had to be ready to jump on board. It didn't take us long to decide. We had already decided that if we were given the opportunity to open Curves in Vanderhoof that we would take it. We would take the first step and make the other important decisions as they came along. Robert wouldn't be able to stay in Kamloops much longer anyway, as 10 years was already longer than most members stayed in one detachment. A northern transfer request was quite likely to be in our favour because not many members wanted to go up north.

It was an exciting day when we signed the papers to accept the Curves offer for the franchise and this was about to totally change our lives once again. A new adventure was coming our way, but if we thought we were busy before, now we were really about to get busy!

Feeling Accomplished!

We signed the papers in February of 2004 and our opening date was for the beginning of July. We lived 7 hours away and there was no sign of a promotion in the works for Robert as of yet. Kayce was graduating in June and this was a big year for her, so I decided to keep working at my current job in the school district until the year ended as well. Colin was in grade 8 and we knew that moving him in high school would be a difficult transition for him. Time was ticking and we had made the decision, so we dug in our heels and started setting our path to how we would accomplish the tasks that lay ahead. We had deadlines to meet with Curves headquarters and needed to travel to Waco, Texas, to be trained in the Curves business, policies and procedures. It was a whirlwind, but we knew we could get the job done. Our opening date was set for the beginning of July and since we both worked full-time, time was of the essence now. We travelled to Vanderhoof every second weekend for months and worked hard from morning till night until we were almost ready to open the doors. We found a place to lease that needed renovating. We built a room for an office and painted the whole place. We needed to buy equipment, office supplies and computers. We needed to advertise and train ourselves to prepare for the big opening day. We were exhausted and hadn't even opened the business yet. Cindy, our oldest daughter, had decided she would come and be my partner for the summer months and help us with the Curves opening. There was a buzz of excitement around the town and women were excited to be getting a gym for women only. What a whirlwind!

Curves Opening

The end of the school year came so fast we thought we had missed spring. Kayce graduated with honors and it was a delight to see our second child finish so well and be ready to enter into the next phase of her life, knowing she was capable of doing whatever she put her mind to. She had decided to go to College in Saskatchewan, much further away than we had hoped, but I had learned with our first child that I needed to let go and let her make her way in the big wide world. I would be very busy with the gym and business details which would help me cope with the empty nest feeling better this time around.

A promotional opportunity had come up in Prince George for Robert and since he had done well on his last promotional exam (all the studying had finally paid off) he applied for the position. He got the position and was actually going to be promoted to Corporal. Wow, 24 years in the RCMP and he was finally moving up in the ranks! I was so proud of him for sticking to it, for achieving a personal goal for himself and getting a good mark on the last promotional exam. It was a blessing in other ways as well. I would be able to live in Prince George and commute back and forth to Vanderhoof to look after the business. Because my parents still lived in Vanderhoof I would just stay with them when the roads were bad and not have to worry about driving in bad weather conditions.

Colin, on the other hand, had just finished grade 8 and he was not impressed to say the least. He was not happy that we were moving him out of Kamloops and that he would not only have to say good-bye to his friends, he would also have to say good-bye to his sister who was leaving the nest. The two of them had become very close over the past year as they attended the same high school, so losing her and moving away from familiarity was going to be especially hard on him.

At the end of June Cindy and I headed out to Vanderhoof to finish up with the last of the training, hiring, and advertising that needed to be done before the opening day at Curves. It was such an exciting time and Cindy and I worked hard from early morning to late at night. We found a little place in Vanderhoof that was in need of a house sitter for a few months, so we were lucky enough to have a quiet place to reprieve to at the end of a long day.

Opening week was absolutely crazy. Curves International had told us that opening week would be controlled chaos and that was no lie! All five of us were involved for the first few weeks and we had a wonderful time working together as a family and seeing our business flourish. We signed up a lot of members in the first 2 weeks and with the girls and I working on training clients on the equipment, my mom helping with traffic control, Robert and Colin entering data onto the computer, we actually were quite well organized and did amazingly well. We had accomplished our goals and done even better than we anticipated.

Robert, Kayce and Colin went back to Kamloops after 2 weeks and Cindy and I stayed in town to run the gym. Bob kept on working and got our house listed on the market, while Colin went to volunteer at a kids' camp for the rest of the summer. Kayce was working at a restaurant serving, which would help to pay for her education in the fall. We were all spread out in different directions and the roller coaster was moving fast.

July and August were a blur at the gym. Life was fast paced and we were doing well. We loved the comradery at the gym and we were building friendships. Helping women achieve their personal goals was very satisfying on a personal level. Life was busy and fun, but by the end of the summer Robert was really tired of having to make the 7 hour drive every second weekend to see me. We were ready to have the house sell and have a normal family life once again. We needed each other and depended on each other far more than we realized. We decided to enroll Colin in an online school program for grade 9 so that he could come up with Bob to see me on the weekends and be able to do his school work from anywhere. This would allow his semester courses to be transferred easily as well.

Cindy was my manager and right hand woman and I was really going to miss having her around at the gym when she had to go back to school. We had so much fun working together and made memories that would last a lifetime. In early September she headed back to UBC in Vancouver, and I already couldn't wait until Christmas when she would be home to work with me again. We made a really good team!

Packing Kayce up for college was another milestone in our lives. As we drove across the prairies and dropped her off at her room in the dorm with strangers surrounding her, tears filled our eyes as another child flew the coop. The goodbye was quick, but tears flowed for miles down the highway. These were difficult times for me and the older I got the more I admired and appreciated my own parents. Funny how, with each passing day, time and life experiences make us just a little wiser.

Move to PG in December

By the end of October our house sold and life would finally normalize somewhat for us again. Robert and Colin came up to Prince George for our house hunting trip and we decided on buying a house on the west side of town so that my commute to Vanderhoof would be a bit shorter on a daily basis. We bought a new house that still had a few weeks' worth of finishing to be done before we were able to move in. We ended up staying in a hotel for about 3 weeks, which gave us a chance to sit and soak in the hot tub and relax before the labour of moving and unpacking once again. It was nice to have Colin around and he often came to Vanderhoof with me on those days, as he could do his online schooling wherever he was.

As it happened, the moving truck was scheduled to unload our things on December 23. We made sure our beds were set up and the coffee pot was out before we went to bed that night. On Christmas Eve, we unpacked until noon and then decided that it was time to celebrate Christmas. The girls had made it home and we were delighted to all pack into our vehicle and head to my parent's house for Christmas. Grandma's house was always a fun time at Christmas time and this year would be no different.

Standing up for Yourself

I think that our time in Prince George was probably the worst place for Robert workwise, but a good place and time for our relationship. It was where we found joy in doing something together that created a bond we will never forget. It was definitely the best place for me workwise, so far in our marriage, and we found good friends in the shortest period of time of all the places we lived. Colin, however, struggled with our first year in Prince George. When his first semester was over, at the end of January, he decided to go back to school so he could meet some kids his own age and try to make friends to hang out with. He was very angry with us for quite some time for moving him to a new place. His loneliness was unbearable at times and I really questioned whether we had made the right decision this time. I loved the Curves business and Robert needed a promotion in his career and yet we asked ourselves if our triumphs and victories were worth making our son so miserable? He couldn't wait until summertime so he could go back to volunteer at camp again and be with his good friends.

Robert was busy for the first year in Prince George trying to learn his job as a Corporal. I was very busy at the gym, commuting back and forth to Vanderhoof most days, and Colin had started in a private high school where he was beginning to make friends. We found a community church to attend and one of the first mornings there we met a couple who were also new to PG and who soon became lifetime friends. Moving to a new place usually requires quite the effort from both parties in building relationships, but this friendship took no effort at all. It was like we were kindred spirits and this made our years in Prince George unforgettable. We also made new friends and connected with old friends from my college years, so Prince George became a place where we built strong relationships.

Robert's work environment in Prince George, however, was quite toxic for a time and the stress levels for him were increasing. It was hard to fight an up-hill battle for too long and it was hard for me to totally understand the whole picture. The RCMP rank structure has its good points and bad points and sometimes I didn't tolerate the political red tape too well. I liked things to be fair and just and, in a world of egotistical type A personalities, this was undoubtedly quite hard to manage. Things all came to a head one day and I remember the day well. I came home from doing errands to find Robert at home in his civilian clothes at a very unusual time. He began to inform me that he was not going to be working in that toxic environment any longer and that he had had enough! He had gone upstairs to the "big guy" and had a little chat that morning. He had told him that someone was going to be leaving that day, either himself or the other guy, but until a decision was made he would be at home and the Staff Sergeant could phone him when he made the decision.

There comes a point in a person's life when you decide that you have had enough of something and you decide to stand up for yourself. This was the day for Robert. Of course, as his wife, hearing this was not the easiest thing in the world to take in. What did this mean? Did this mean we were moving, or that he was going on stress leave, or that he would be told to go back to work and suck it up? I had no idea what to expect and so my life was hanging in the balance as well. Consequences for actions taken by a spouse affect the other partner equally as much only the feelings of the partner are just brushed aside. The only thing that matters at that moment is to try to be a support and figure things out together.

It wasn't long before Robert received a phone call to come back down to the office for a chat with his superior officer. Things needed to proceed and so I was left to wait in suspense as my husband went in to work things out. The issues were resolved fairly quickly as a result of his actions and this proved to make his job more tolerable for the moment. Robert was one to stand up for what he believed was right, and when he felt things weren't right, he was not one to sit by and watch it happen. His quote to live by was this: "The only thing necessary for the triumph of evil is for good men to do nothing." (Edmund Burke). This helped him deal with many confrontational issues in his career.

Something to Do Together

The gym was doing well and we were finally actually making a bit of extra cash. Robert's raise in pay with the promotion was also helping us financially and so we decided to splurge a bit on the two of us. We found a motorbike that Bob really liked, a Victory Touring Cruiser, and decided to spend some of our hard earned cash on this. He had been riding the RCMP Harley for quite a few years now, both in Kamloops and in Prince George, and he preferred the Victory over the Harley. It was a happy day for Robert when he got to take his new bike home.

Over the next few months we started to look for a bike for me. I had decided that if we were going to ride together, then I wanted to have my own bike as well and not always be on the back of his. We started looking for a smaller bike and soon found one that was just perfect for me. I needed a bike that had been lowered because of my height and it wasn't long before we found a Honda Shadow that fit me just perfectly. I remember my first ride with great pride. It was exhilarating and empowering and the first of many enjoyable rides to come. Robert and I had looked for something enjoyable that we could do together for a long time and we had finally found our thing. We thoroughly enjoyed our outings riding together, which also helped relieve stress, but more importantly we felt a strong connection of true friendship as we rode together side by side.

How Things Change

The summer after we moved to Prince George proved to be an exciting time as our daughter, Cindy, and her high-school sweetheart, Andres, decided to get married. They were both planning on becoming teachers and would now be married students for a few years together. Cindy and I worked together at Curves and had fun planning her wedding in our spare time. Her father and I knew she was ready to leave our nest for good and everything came together smoothly, almost effortlessly. She was a lovely beautiful bride and we didn't lose a daughter, we gained a son-in-law.

Kayce had decided to transfer schools after a year and a half so we were able to have her at home for a few months. She ended up having to transfer soon again and finish up her degree at TRU in Kamloops. After graduating with a degree in Human Resource Management, Kayce landed a job in an HR department in Langley, BC so she was starting her career and having to move again.

Colin had settled into Prince George quite well, especially after he got his driver's license and could get himself to and from the golf course by himself. He spent as much time as he could on the golf courses and it seemed like we blinked and suddenly he was graduating from high school. How could our last child be leaving already! He had decided to fly the coop as well and attend university in Langley so he would be sharing accommodations with his sister, which made him leaving a little more bearable for us.

These last 5 years had brought immeasurable changes in our lives. We could hardly keep up with the way things were progressing. The train was moving and instead of slowing down it was speeding up.

Selling the Business and Moving on

Robert had done his time as a Corporal and it was time for him to start applying for Sergeant. We needed him to get one more raise so that his pension would reflect a higher salary for his best 5 years. He started writing the promotional exams again and now that he knew how to prepare for them, he wasn't troubled by them.

We both knew when we opened Curves that it would be for a short time, as our long-term goal had always been for Robert to finish 35 years in the RCMP. I had put my career path on hold for him and for us to own Curves, for just a few short years, was all I needed to fulfil my dream of owning a business. It had been an extremely happy time in my life when I could concentrate on something for me and I loved the workout, the ladies, the staff and the energy, but it was time to look for a buyer and move on in our RCMP career. I say our career because I felt like I was married to the RCMP as well.

It wasn't long before I sold the gym to my manager, a lady who I still hold dear to my heart, and it was with great sadness that I said good-bye to the life of Curves. I knew that I would have to fill the void with something immediately as I had built up so many relationships that fed my soul. It was my passion and I loved helping and serving people. I would truly miss my business.

I immediately invested in a 3-month training program to become a nail technician so that I had a reason to get up every day. I made myself get out rather than sit at home and feel sorry for myself. Three months later I received my certificate and got a job in a spa working part-time. I needed to fill my days with something so I wouldn't get depressed and down in the dumps. I essentially went from owner to slave, as I call it, which was very hard indeed and yet fulfilled its purpose. To be an owner that put my heart and soul into my business and then switch to working for someone who was quite the opposite was very hard to comprehend. I trudged on though knowing that I had to get over the fact that Curves was no longer mine. I was moving on.

How to Survive the Ride?

As I have said before, the only thing constant in life is change – how we accept the change is what makes our life easy or difficult. In the last 5 years we had so many learning opportunities that came our way and helped to make us who we are today. I found that doing things together with Bob, activities that we both enjoyed, was crucial in surviving the ride! Taking up motor-biking together was one of those rejuvenating things that helped us relieve stress and feel a sense of oneness that helped us survive the ride.

Chapter 6
A Step Up in The Ladder of Success

Promotion to Sergeant in Williams Lake

Thankfully it didn't take too long with me working in the spa before Robert got the promotion he so desperately needed. He was promoted to Sergeant of Traffic Services in Williams Lake and he needed this raise in pay so that our pension would be okay when he retired from the RCMP. I was able to quit my job at the spa and now another new chapter in our life was about to begin. Time for another new town, new house, new job and new friends but a very different move because this time we were moving without any children. We were really empty nesters now and life would be totally different in so many ways. Our lives were always centered around our children previously and now for the first time in 25 years, life would be centered on just the two of us. My life with a cop would now change in ways that I never even imagined. What would these next 5 years before retirement hold for us? Surely we didn't know, but for now my hubby was about to become the Sergeant in charge and I was just a tad bit proud of him!

House Hunting Again

We looked forward to our house hunting trip this time. We had searched online and found a few houses that looked interesting but some were a bit out of our price range. Robert would be getting a substantial raise in pay as Sergeant so maybe we could afford a few more luxuries this time. We were middle-aged and had done alright in our 65-year plan of life, or so we thought at the time! We set up an appointment with the realtor and thought we were ready to go. We had done this a few times before and knew how taxing these days could be. There was a lot to look at, lots to think about, lots of decisions to make and lots of priorities to put into perspective. We discussed what we really wanted in a house, what we could do without and still be happy with, what our price point was, whether we wanted a house that needed renovating or one that was completely finished, the size of house, which side of town we wanted to live in etc. etc.

We arrived in Williams Lake in the afternoon and went to the realtor's office to let them know that we had made it to town. We decided on a time to meet the next morning for coffee to discuss all our wants and needs and then spent the rest of the evening driving around getting familiar with the area and checking out the RCMP station. The following morning we were ready to roll. The realtor had pulled up quite a few listings in our price range and had a full day planned for us. He had been recommended to us, had a good reputation in town, and we felt comfortable with him. Now the one thing that is very important to me in buying a house is for the realtor to listen to both my husband and I, not just my husband! I had found a house online that I had wanted to look at but looking through the listings printed off I didn't see this particular house. I mentioned this fact to the realtor but he just said that he had pulled up listings in the price range that Robert had given him. That would be okay for today, I thought, and we would have another look later on that night. Was this quiet spoken realtor going to work for me? That I didn't know quite yet.

We had a full day driving around and looking at many different properties and most of them we knew right off that they wouldn't work for us. Our big wants were a good size garage and a house that was big enough for all of our kids to come home at the same time and each have a place to sleep. I wanted an open floor plan with a nice kitchen but we really weren't too fussy, we thought.

At the end of the day we had found one house that we sort of liked and yet it needed quite a bit of renovating before we could live there comfortably. I mentioned the house I had seen online to the realtor again and he didn't really know which one I meant, so he drove us around to look at a few different neighbourhoods. The last neighbourhood he took us to I saw the house I liked and requested a viewing of that particular house. He said it was not in the price range that we had given him but I told him I would like to see it anyway. He didn't really say too much more about it and as he dropped us off at the end of the day, I wondered if he would show it to us the next day.

That night we pondered about all that had transpired and I mentioned to Robert that if the realtor did not show us the house we wanted to see the next day, we might have to switch realtors. So far we had seen one house that we would consider making an offer on and we went to bed wondering which house would be ours.

The next morning as we met for coffee again, I was thoroughly impressed with the realtor as he handed me the listings he had for us to view that day. To my surprise, the first listing to view for the day was the house I really wanted to see! Suddenly he now had my full trust and respect and I would be ready to purchase a house with this realtor, regardless of which one it was. He had heard and listened to me.

As we entered the door of this house Robert and I looked at each other and knew instantly that this was the house we wanted. It had the open concept design, a nice kitchen, hard-wood floors, a huge garage, and a great view of the lake! What more could we ask for? It was a little out of our price range but we decided that it would be worth our while to spend a little extra and love where we lived. After a bit of negotiating, we settled on a price and eventually this house became ours.

New Job for Me Again

We moved into our new house just off the highway in Williams Lake the beginning of July. It was my favourite house because I loved the wrap around balcony with a view that overlooked the lake. I enjoyed many peaceful hours over the 6 years there, sitting outside on the deck drinking my coffee and lying in the sun. Of course, I needed to find another job so that I could help contribute to our financial affairs and so I ended up fulfilling another dream of mine, which was to become a medical transcriptionist. I applied to take a one-year course online and thought that the first year in Williams Lake would be a great time to spend studying as I didn't know a soul! I have a gift of being able to focus or rather retreat into a new task and so I plunged in hook, line and sinker. I spent more hours on this course than I would have working a full-time job, but it gave me a sense of fulfillment and kept me busy while Robert was getting to know his new role as Sergeant. I enjoyed the course, frustrating as it was at times, and before the year was up I had been hired on by the hospital on a casual basis to do medical transcription. I was extremely fortunate because transcription jobs were very hard to come by, especially just fresh out of school.

Empty Nest

Moving to Williams Lake from Prince George took a little bit of adjusting. Williams Lake had almost everything we needed in terms of shopping, but it was only about a quarter of the size of PG. We also had not been alone for 25 years – a quarter of a century – which was another adjustment that we had to make. Because Colin, our youngest child, had lived at camp for the past five summers, the empty nest syndrome wasn't as hard as we thought it would be. The vacant feeling in the summers helped to normalize the empty feeling now. We had our motor-biking hobby that we indulged in now. There were many little one hour rides we could take after a long day of work for Robert and a long day of studying for me. Robert and I would usually go and practice very slow driving before we headed out on a ride. We would head off into a parking lot and practice, practice, practice. We practiced circles, the closer the better, riding lines, turning sharp, following the leader, and quick stops etc. It is so much harder to ride slow than fast, and I always loved a challenge. We loved these little one to two hour trips after work, the feeling of freedom, the smells of nature, the sights of God's creation, the unity of us riding side by side, togetherness, just the two of us.

Togetherness

Togetherness is wonderful but there comes a time when I need more than just the two of us. I need female companionship, couple friends, going out in groups, having people over and having friends to go for coffee with etc. What I was finding was that I was really missing our good friends in Prince George and I was lonely. We found friends so fast in Prince George and luckily we were only two and a half hours down the road from them so we could hop in the car and visit on the weekends easily.

With Robert being Sergeant now, I was experiencing that people were treating us differently than when he was Corporal or just a lowly Constable. How odd, we were the same people! I remember the day when I actually realized that we were not just Robert and Ruth any more, but we were Sergeant (Boss) and the boss's wife. One of the guys working for Robert came to the house one day and what he said to me really opened my eyes. He was very respectful and didn't really want to come in for a visit and suddenly it dawned on me! My husband was the Boss! We were management now and the comradery would be very different because of this. For the members working under Robert, we would always be the boss and the boss's wife here, not just Robert and Ruth. I also began to notice that others in the community also treated us with just a bit more respect than before. This was a weird phenomenon to me and I started noticing this more and more as we were out and about in the community.

Because of this, it was now extra important to find friends that didn't treat us differently and who would just get to know us as Robert and Ruth and not Sergeant Verbree and the Sergeant's wife. Togetherness was good, but not enough.

New Biker Friends

We found a church to attend in town, as we usually did wherever we lived, and this time we picked a church where we felt we should get involved and be of some service to the congregation. We were hoping to meet some people that might become good friends as well and looked forward to getting to know people in the community. This church had a small congregation of maybe 150 attendees and so it shouldn't be too hard to get to know some people our own age in our stage of life with adult children, we thought.

In the next week or so, I received a phone call from a woman inviting me out for coffee. How encouraging, I thought, that someone would reach out to me like this. Through the following months and years to come, we connected and would meet regularly to share and counsel each other about the day to day struggles we both were facing. Our lives have become entwined through other relationships as well and it is interesting to see how God works out his plan for our lives.

I was away one Sunday visiting my parents soon after we started attending this church, so Robert went to church by himself and met a fellow biker and his wife. They invited him out for lunch where he met some of their other friends, another couple who were also bikers. Robert was excited to tell me about his lunch out with these bikers because the one particular couple were some of the most unlikely people for Bob to become friends with, and yet they hit it off immediately. Now Robert, amongst other policemen in his age bracket, was a cop who thought that most people who had tattoos were bad apples. There were always the exceptions, of course, but for the most part Robert would not normally associate with people who were covered in tattoos. Now I'm not talking about a few little tattoos on the ankles, arms or backs; I am talking about tattoos that cover the body or a good portion of the body. From his description of this guy, who was covered in tattoos, I was not sure what to think either but I looked forward to the next Sunday with anticipation when I would meet these people too.

Sure enough, the next Sunday we were again invited to join them for lunch immediately after church and this lunch outing was the beginning of another beautiful friendship. We had a wonderful visit with them where they welcomed us with open arms. We were not the boss or the boss's wife to them, just plain old Bob and Ruth. This was somewhat comforting to me because I didn't want to be excluded from friendships just because my husband was the boss and they felt they had to be careful what they said around me. The tattoos were a little astonishing to me as well, although very artistic, but the fact that Bob thought he was a great guy was what perplexed me the most. His eyes were being opened; he was stepping outside of his comfort zone and taking a risk with this tattooed biker. We sat and visited for a long time that day and soon planned to meet again. What we encountered that day was truly precious, true friendship. I know that true friendship is often hard to find when you move around in your career, but it is so wonderful when you have someone you can totally trust and confide in. The older I get the more precious relationships become. It's not about the outward appearance, but all about the heart and this was a lesson that we both were learning more and more. These new friends helped us learn this in a whole new way.

How to Survive the Ride?

To survive the ride in my life with a cop I needed to have something in my life in each location that was strictly for myself, in this case it was the transcription course which gave me a purpose and helped me focus on something totally different than RCMP life. I was my own person too and needed to use the gifts and talents that I had been dealt; I had to be an individual and have my own life, apart from my husband's so that we were a little more rounded in life. We had decided together to fulfil his dream of being in the RCMP for a lifetime career and yet along that pathway I had to have my own joy and fulfilment in life, which meant looking after my wants and needs as well. In order to survive the ride, I needed to be my own person and have my own identity outside of being known as just a cop's wife.

Chapter 7
Life in Williams Lake

Sharing Hopes and Dreams

Robert was beginning to get the hang of his new job as Sergeant, which proved to be a lot more of a challenge than he expected. He was put into a position where he had to really paddle uphill for quite some time and go against the flow before he got his unit to where it should be. This was not a popularity contest or an award winning competition, but it was necessary to have his unit be the best it could be. These struggles were a challenge, but Robert wasn't afraid to stand up for what was right and go against the higher ranked men to make the changes that were necessary. As hard as this was, Robert did a great job and I think it was always a little harder emotionally for me than for him. It takes time to make these kinds of changes, but Robert had the stick-to-itiveness that was required of such a task.

The little boys' club, as the outside world knows it, was a phrase we used often as well. It is usually who you know, not what you know, and there is a lot of backstabbing that goes on when you have a bunch of type A personalities working together. Throughout Robert's career we saw this play out in many different scenarios. Regardless, Robert was a cop through and through and for the most part he always loved going to work. It was the right career for him and we were making our way.

We did have aspirations, hopes and dreams, and I especially really hoped that Robert would become a Staff Sergeant before he retired. He had worked so hard for the federal government. He really did give his life to serve his country and yet this dream was not to be. He did apply for a few positions that came up in the later years, but because of the way the little boys' club works, this was not to be. Robert was okay with this, as he had lived a life time with it already, and yet the politics that go on amongst the ranks would drive me around the bend. We all have to realize that some dreams do come true, but not all of them, and this was one that was not going to be realized.

Home for the Summer

We began to adjust to our new life in Williams Lake, found our little niche and settled in quite nicely. Our first Christmas would be different here because our kids would all come home and wouldn't know a soul! That meant that they would be bored silly, be housebound and want to leave town quickly. As it happened, I was right. They all came home and only stayed for a few days. The good thing was that we could also skip town and go visit our friends, which is just what we did.

That summer our son got a job in Williams Lake and ended up home with us in the summer for the first time in years. He was going to university and needed to make some money; therefore, camp was out of the question for the time being. It was wonderful to have him home and even though he didn't have friends in town, he worked during the week and was close enough to both cities, Kamloops and Prince George, to be able to visit his friends and golf on the weekends. It was great for him to be home this summer because he ended up learning to ride motorbike too and the three of us could go out for rides after work together. It was a good bonding time for father and son and it was nice to see them enjoying some adult activities together. Our three children were now all adults and we had to learn to get to know each one as a friend and not just as a son or daughter. Relationships change as we let go of the strings attached to each one, this is easier said than done, and we are still learning to do this today in many ways.

Not Ready to be Grandma!

The following year, late in the fall, we received a package in the mail from our oldest daughter. She was an artist who had come up with a series of paintings called The Wobbles. These paintings were very bright and playful canvases and she had quite the collection already. She had let us know that we could expect something in the mail soon and that we should call her when it arrived. As we unwrapped the brown paper package, with her on the phone, we pulled out a canvas of a Wobble baking a bun in the oven! Wow – what a message! I was going to be a Grandma! This particular surprise message was another big game changer in the game of life. We would be grandparents in the spring!

The shock wore off after a few weeks, but then once it sunk in I wondered if I was really ready to be a Grandma. I was finally used to the empty nest and was feeling good about not having to worry about our children all the time or be responsible for someone else, and now we were going to be grandparents. I was really excited for my daughter, but I wasn't ready to be a Grandma yet; I rode a motorbike!

Another Beautiful Wedding

During this year we also had another fantastic event happening in our life! Our second daughter got engaged and we began planning for that wonderful day. Kayce was working and living in Langley, we were living in Williams Lake and yet she was going to be married in Prince George and then move to Edmonton right after the wedding. It was certainly a bit confusing for people. She was marrying Kevin, a blue collar worker who had just gotten a good job in Edmonton, so they were going to be settling in Alberta. She had found her life partner in Prince George while she was at home working for the summer, and eventually, after a bit of a bumpy relationship, they decided they were meant for each other and were going to tie the knot. They decided on a winter wedding and plans were coming along nicely. The wedding came together without too many hitches and soon we were blessed to have another son-in-law in the family. It was a very snowy day in early January and it truly was a winter wonderland wedding.

We felt blessed to have two children now who were well on their way to making their own way in life. Kayce had graduated from university with a business degree and Cindy had graduated with an education degree, so they were both set, at least as set as most parents could hope for. They both had the resources to look after themselves if they needed to, which was a goal of ours in raising children. Since I had given up my career in the bank to get married and support my hubby in his career as a cop, our goal was to have our children be able to support themselves, if they should ever need to. Times were often quite tough for us financially because I didn't have a career to fall back on, and we really didn't want this for our children's future. Times were getting tougher financially, not easier, and most couples now needed two incomes to survive the debt load.

Reality of a Sick Parent

It was also during this year that we realized that my mother was starting to go downhill. We had noticed that she was getting more anxious and was starting to get forgetful. The time came when we had to face reality. Appointments were made with a geriatric team and she was diagnosed with Alzheimer's. This was not a good diagnosis and she didn't really want to hear it. She was in denial which made things even more difficult. My poor mother had looked after my father for all these years and now she was losing ground. How were we ever going to face this dreadful disease?

The doctors said that we had time and that there was no need to make decisions hastily. But things needed to be discussed and my mom needed to make a plan on how to go forward in the future. This was hard for her and she really couldn't face the facts. She looked after her husband and she just wasn't ready to hear it.

A Baby Granddaughter

The following June our little granddaughter arrived safe and sound. We waited in anticipation as our daughter went from trying to deliver naturally to having an emergency C-section, which made us just a little bit nervous for a few hours. As I sat in the hospital awaiting the outcome, I was so thankful that her doctor saw me and gently came and reassured me that everything would be just fine. Our daughter was having a baby, was in distress, and as a mother it was one of the hardest things I had to let go of. They had decided they wanted to do this on their own, not understanding the depth of concern of a parent yet themselves, and I needed to let go and respect their desires. Letting go of things is sometimes easy and sometimes difficult, and this was one of those difficult times for both Robert and I. Our children grow up and become their own person, different from us, and we have to allow them this privilege as they have their life to live just as we have ours to live.

Our grand-daughter arrived with 10 fingers and 10 toes and we were so blessed to be able to hold this precious little angel. Grandchildren are truly a gift from God and all my thoughts about not being ready to be a Grandma faded as our hearts melted and welcomed this little bundle into our family without hesitation.

Camping With Friends

We now were on the road more than ever with a grandchild in Kamloops, friends in Prince George, a daughter and son-in-law in Edmonton and our son still down the valley in Langley going to university.

We felt like we were never home and maybe that contributed to us feeling like we weren't really connecting with too many people in Williams Lake. We had become close with our biker friends and a few other couples, and we all started talking about going camping together. We used to camp every summer when the kids were smaller but hadn't camped now for quite a few years. We started looking at different trailers and soon got the bug again. We did a lot of trailer shopping and Robert did a lot of research on which trailer to buy. We finally settled on one that we both liked, a new 24-foot, rear kitchen unit that we were very pleased with. We were set to go camping again and we loaded up and headed off to try it out. This was our type of camping, in a trailer with all the amenities. We appreciate having our own kitchen, having our own bathroom and shower and staying at campgrounds that have water, sewer and electricity. Setting up, cooking, cleaning and washing dishes, doing laundry etc. can all be considered work, but somehow in the world of camping these tasks don't seem quite as laborious as they do at home, especially when you are doing it with friends.

Our camping trips were a lot of fun the next few years and we saw quite a few miles put on our truck and trailer. Camping was another activity that Robert and I enjoyed doing together and helped break up the monotony of day to day work life in the summer months.

Son Joins the Military

After two years of university in Langley, our son transferred back to Kamloops to finish his Computer Science degree. He then applied to the Military and was accepted into the Officer Cadet Program to become an air traffic controller. This meant that right after graduation he was sent to Basic Training which would prove to be quite difficult. We were so excited for him to join the Military, and we were told that he would be part of the new generation that would help to change the face of the Military the way we knew it to be. We were very proud of our son who was joining an organization where he would be serving our country as Robert had served the country. There is some weird sense of patriotic pride that one feels when you serve in such a capacity and both Robert and I felt this now for our son.

How to Survive the Ride?

I believe that to survive the ride we must face the storms of life by hitting them head on. Sometimes the storms are mild, while other times they are fierce, but going through them head on and dealing with them rather than ignoring them makes you grow as a person. Robert had to face his challenges at work and they were not easy. We were working through hardships with our adult children and I had to face my own challenges as well, starting another new career at the age of 50. This was not an easy task I must say, but Robert encouraged me through my storms as I encouraged him through his and together we faced them head on. He would listen to me complain about my frustrations and I would get him to open up and talk about his. Keeping all that stuff bottled up inside is not healthy, so our walking made us talk and clear the air and we continued to face each storm as it came.

Chapter 8
Time to Release

Married Kids Move Home

Our kids are often our biggest challenge and rightfully so. They are a part of us and when they are hurting we are hurting too. When they are excited, we are excited. When they accomplish something great, we are proud of them. When they need something, we try to give it to them. When they laugh, we laugh with them and when they cry, we cry alongside them.

Half way through our time in Williams Lake, Kayce and her husband, Kevin, relocated from Edmonton back to Prince George. Kayce had been unable to find a human resource job in Edmonton and Kevin had been promised a good welding job in Prince George, so they decided being closer to family would be in their best interest. Unfortunately, this did not seem to work out like they were promised and so they found themselves looking for jobs in Williams Lake. Kevin had applied to get into the RCMP, which Robert was thrilled about, and since it was a 2-year process we told them they could live with us during this waiting time if they so desired. This would help them get back on their feet again financially, so to speak, and Kayce could live with us while Kevin would be at depot for 6 months of training. During this 2-year waiting time Kevin had to meet many requirements in the whole hiring process, and he met every one with flying colours. He was given a regimental number and this, we thought, meant he was ready to go. Finally, after almost 2 years of waiting and putting his life on hold, he was told that he would be in the next troop or the one after that. During this whole process, Kevin worked as a welder at the mine and got more experience in his field of expertise. He was a red seal welder, so that served him well while he was waiting on the RCMP process.

During this two-year process Kevin was told to continue on with his life as close to normal as possible because if he failed any part of the testing, he would be out of the running. It is hard to put your life on hold for two years waiting for a certain career, but they tried to resume a normal life style. They decided to start a family regardless of whether Kevin would be home or at depot in training, and they would just have to rearrange things as they transpired. Kayce became pregnant soon after their decision to start a family and they were so delighted with this news. Eight weeks later, unfortunately, Kayce ended up miscarrying and started on a downward spiral herself. She had been so excited to have a baby and then to lose it so quickly was a real loss. You get your hopes up so much and then suddenly they are snatched away. This was more devastating to her than we imagined it would be. I had never had a miscarriage myself and I had never grieved for an unborn child. It was hard on all of us, but watching our daughter ache was even more painful. Her sister, on the other hand, was pregnant again and was about to have her second child and all was going well with her. It was so hard to change faces and be happy for one daughter, but be grieving for the other about the same subject, children. Life wasn't fair.

About two days before Christmas, Kevin received a phone call that changed their lives again. After passing all the tests and jumping through all the hoops, having received his regimental number and being told he would be in the next troop, he was now told that it was all over. He would not be going to depot and was not being hired by the RCMP! No explanation, not a clue about why he was not accepted; only that he would not be going. This was a real shock to all of us and Robert was especially appalled. The RCMP were in desperate need of recruits and here was a great man willing to serve our country who had passed all the tests and now was turned down without an explanation! Totally appalling!

The candle flickered and the flame dimmed for Robert that day in the RCMP. The life of the RCMP was changing and it was just about time for us to get out. Kevin and Kayce would rebound; they were young and resilient but this was a discouraging time as they had put their life on hold for 2 years. They needed to come up with plan B, but at least they weren't in a panic, as Kevin had a good paying job at the moment. It was time to set a different course to their sail.

Living with married kids is a new experience altogether. It's hard to give up your space once you have adjusted to the empty nest, and yet we all managed to live together under one roof without too many disagreements. We all had to decide to make it work and do our part, which we did, and Robert and I were given the chance to get to know Kevin on a much deeper level which has also enriched our lives. We are so thankful for the time we had with them in Williams Lake.

Second Grandchild, Second Miscarriage, Life isn't Fair

We were blessed to have another grand-daughter born in February of 2012. I was fortunate enough to be able to go down to Kamloops and help look after our first little angel, as number two grand-daughter was being born. Cindy ended up having another emergency caesarean section and so mom and baby remained in hospital for three days to recuperate. It was a blessing to see this little precious miracle and to be able to enjoy some time getting to know and bond with our little grand-daughters.

As wonderful as this was for Cindy, it was equally as hard for Kayce, as she so far had not been able to have children. She had conceived again but was unable to carry to full term and lost the baby again at around 8 weeks into the pregnancy. Life certainly wasn't fair and it was very hard to be so thrilled for one daughter and yet so deeply saddened for the other daughter. What would life hold for Kayce, who so desperately wanted to be a mother like her other family, friends and relatives. This hardship was not over yet but she would manage to not just go through the storm, but to grow through the storm.

Right Time to Retire

When you get to the age of retirement from a pensionable job it is good to consider all the pros and cons of how and when to actually retire. Informative retirement courses are set up to help you figure out how to get the most bang for your buck and to help you figure out the best date and time of year to actually retire. Robert went to a few of these courses and he had some representative help him figure out that the best time for him to retire would be July 23, 2014. That would put him at his goal of accomplishing 35 years in the RCMP and having served his country to the best of his ability, yet still capable of doing something else after retiring from the Force.

After help with figuring out the details, Robert signed the release documents and his retirement date was set! There was actually going to be an end to our RCMP life and maybe some kind of a new life. Time would tell. For now, Robert was excited about the future and getting out; his cup was full of bureaucracy and it was time to leave the life he knew to try something different.

Because of the way holidays worked in the RCMP, Robert had enough time banked that his last day of work was actually April 11, 2014. The last couple of months went by quickly and we planned and dreamt of things to do after his last day of work so that his transition from being so busy to retiring would go smoothly.

His last week of work was filled with saying good-bye to this life he knew. He had a few retirement lunches and all the political good stuff was said. He was a very hard working individual who served his country well! He did his time and his staff was sorry to see him go. He was excited and a bit nervous all at the same time, after all, 35 years in one career with a close comradery is hard to cut off all at once.

He had already had the office party and now it was time to celebrate with family and friends. We had a lovely celebration party that I put together at our house and almost everyone invited was able to make it. What we realized that day was how fortunate we were. With most of our couple friends, either both or at least one spouse had some serious health issues going on. Robert was 57 when he retired, and I was 54, and our friends were all in our age bracket. We were the only couple who didn't have some kind of health problems. That was astounding to me; we were young and this didn't seem right. These problems included major open heart surgery, hemochromatosis, breast cancer, depression, anxiety, disability due to a serious car crash, the need for a pace-maker, Lyme disease, arthritis and multiple surgeries due to car crashes, amongst other minor issues in comparison. When I gave this some thought, I realized that we had much to be thankful for. We were fortunate to have healthy bodies and could still do whatever we wanted to do. We had a great retirement party and it was so wonderful to celebrate our life in the RCMP.

Losing my Mom

The story continues with my mom. She was going downhill fast with Alzheimer's taking over her body. She was only recognizing me half the time and I was now really just a care-aide to her. She would ask me strange questions that would make me turn away and cry. She would call me Mrs. Bob sometimes and even though I knew she still recognized me, she couldn't put the words together properly. We would argue about silly things and I would tell myself to stop and try to laugh about it, but sometimes I just couldn't laugh. We were told to find humour in the situation and that was easy at times, but very difficult at other times. She was still such a caring, loving person and she would want to stop and talk to everyone she met, but I just wanted to have my mom back.

In the midst of these hardships with my mom, Kayce was expecting again for the third time and we were truly hoping for a miracle for her. Surely God would give her a child to hold in her arms this time. How could she possibly survive another pregnancy loss? She tried not to become excited and tried to remain distant from her true feelings of desire. She wanted to remain neutral in light of the fact that she could miscarry again. We were all hopeful!

Robert's last full day of work before holidays was April 11, 2014. On this Friday he had to go to Prince George to hand in some of his RCMP paraphernalia and say goodbye to his boss. That day we arranged to have an anniversary lunch for my parents in Prince George. My aunt and uncle drove them in and had lunch with us as well as a few other people I had invited. They were celebrating 57 years of marriage and that was something to celebrate. This particular day, my mom was really there; her mind was clear. She knew me as her daughter and she was enjoying the lunch and the celebration of their anniversary. We had such a good visit and we went away from the restaurant that day with a very fond memory, which would prove to be our last.

Robert and I stayed with friends in Prince George that night and we reminisced about how well my mom was that day. The next day we drove home to Williams Lake and walked in the door at approximately 8 o'clock in the evening. Around 9 o'clock the phone rang which changed our lives drastically again. My aunt phoned to tell me that she had bad news; my mom, who was being cared for by the paramedics, had just fallen down a flight of 14 stairs and was unconscious. I was numb! I had just had the most wonderful luncheon with her the day before celebrating Mom and Dad's anniversary, and now she was unconscious and things looked really grave. They would be transferring her out to Prince George Hospital that night and my brother would meet the ambulance at the hospital. I would come the following morning.

The next morning we packed up again and headed back to Prince George. Mom had survived the night, but the doctors didn't give us any hope. She had multiple skull fractures that would not be amenable to any treatment. Eventually they put her on comfort measures and transferred her back to Vanderhoof hospital where she could be around family and friends. She survived 5 days in hospital but never did wake up. These were some of the hardest days I have endured. Saying goodbye to my mom and seeing her lying there was a lot to take in. We all had time to say what we needed to, love her to the end, and say our heartfelt goodbyes. I had the best mom a girl could ever wish for and life would never be the same for me after she passed.

After all the hurt of losing my mom, my poor darling daughter had to experience the loss of yet another miscarriage. No one knew she was losing a child, except for her husband and her dad and I. As we grieved the loss of my mom together, saying goodbye and asking my mom to care for her three little great grandchildren in heaven was heart wrenching. We are told to be thankful in all situations and we were thankful that Kayce could openly grieve for the loss of her child, even though no one would understand the depth of her grieving, and that my mom would be up there loving these three little babies ever so much.

In the back of my mind I knew we needed to look at this whole scenario with my mom as a blessing in disguise. Her doctor told us that, as horrible as this was, she didn't suffer and was still able to leave with her dignity intact, unlike many other Alzheimer patients. Although there was comfort in knowing she had no pain and that she didn't have to survive what would have been the horrible years of Alzheimer's, the pain of having her gone went deep. My mom was my mentor and dearest friend, my hero, my soul mate and she had gone through all the ups and downs of my life with a cop. I would miss her deeply and forever.

Renovating a House

To help Robert with adjusting to not going to work every day we had made plans to go and help our son renovate his house in Moose Jaw, Saskatchewan. This was a big project, much bigger than we had originally anticipated, and the catch was that there was a deadline because he had some roommates moving in on a certain date. Due to the unfortunate circumstances with my mother, we were now behind a few weeks of renovating time. Our good friends from Williams Lake offered to come and help us for a few weeks and this was a huge blessing to us. Not only would we have a lot of fun together, but the work would get done much quicker and put us back on schedule.

We arrived in Moose Jaw at the end of April, late in the day. It was getting dark and the weather was dull and cold. The plan was to put down some mattresses, clean up so that it was livable, and stay in the house while we renovated. As we entered the house and went from room to room, our faces grew more somber and somewhat distressed. We knew this was going to be a big project but this was way more than we had bargained for. The whole house was a disaster, to say the least, and the bathrooms were completely disgusting. There was no way we could live in a mess like this and try to prepare meals in a kitchen in such disarray. Robert figured we could still just put down some mattresses and make do, but with friends to help us we couldn't ask them stay in this horrible mess. Robert was a make-do type of man, but with two women who needed to feed working men, we needed proper facilities with a working washroom and working fridge and range. It was time I stepped up to the plate and state that we were not going to stay there. Robert could if he so desired but my friend and I would not! We would go out and find a different place to stay for a few weeks or at least until we had a working kitchen and washroom.

My friend and I left the house to go find a hotel room while the men stayed at the house to decide what course of action to take. They would start first thing in the morning, but first they needed to decide where to begin. The whole house needed renovating and renters were moving in on May 1. We had one month to install new floors throughout the house, paint the kitchen cabinets, put in new counter tops, gut and redo two full bathrooms, paint the whole interior, trim the whole house, have a new heater, hot water tank and air conditioner installed, paint and fix underneath the patio, rip up the cracked, old 8-inch cement slab underneath the patio, clean up the yard, clean up the garage, hall in 12 loads of crushed gravel for the walk and make the house livable. It was a little daunting and overwhelming to say the least. We had just driven 17 hours to get to Moose Jaw and we really just needed something to eat and 8 hours of sleep. Our sense of ha-ha had vanished for now and we needed to regroup and collect our thoughts.

After finding a hotel with a kitchen unit and washrooms that worked, we went back and told the guys what we had found. By this time Robert was okay with my plan so we all headed out for dinner and then crashed in the hotel room that became our home for the next two weeks. Over the course of the next two weeks, we were so thankful that we could come back at the end of a long day and relax in a room that was clean, warm and cozy, where we could put up our feet and have a few laughs. Our friends were truly a blessing as they worked alongside of us and we laughed till we cried and had a great time as we worked our butts off, literally.

At the end of two weeks the house started to look like a home and we were sorry to see our friends leave. We will never forget the time we shared together there. We worked so hard we could barely move at the end of each day. We felt muscles we never knew we had. Working to help someone else gives you a sense of fulfilment that fills your life with purpose. All this hard work was also helping us grieve the loss of my mom. We could release frustrations as we ripped and tore out the old floor. We could let go of anger and bitterness as we threw junk into the big loading garbage bin. We could laugh and cry and work through our sorrow as we reminisced about my mom.

During the last week before our friends were about to leave Moose Jaw, my friend got a phone call from her doctor about an ultrasound that she had before coming out. The news wasn't good; she was diagnosed with breast cancer. Another overwhelming situation!

Two weeks had flown by. Our friends had to travel home and we would remain in Moose Jaw to finish up the renovating with our son. We all checked out of the hotel together and parted ways. This was a hard goodbye as my friend was going home to have to start dealing with her cancer. She felt if she stayed, she could just ignore it, but now it was time to face reality. She had decided that for treatment she was going to do the natural holistic therapy and this was a big learning process as well. As we watched them drive away that day, we felt another hurt that was hard to bear. I had just lost my mom, my daughter Kayce just had her third miscarriage, and now my friend had breast cancer. My hubby had just had his last day of work and this was supposed to be the best time of our lives! It wasn't turning out to be all that it was supposed to be.

We moved our stuff into the house and I felt a loneliness creep in that didn't go away. This was the beginning of a spiraling downward that I will discuss later on. We had so much work to do and it was time to re-focus and make a plan on how we were about to accomplish this goal. We liked goals, so writing our goals down for each day allowed us to complete what we set out to do. At the end of each day we would go over our list of goals and put a strike through the ones that were done. At least this way we could see things carried out and feel like we had accomplished something at the end of a long, tiring day.

Throughout the next month we worked hard day after day, but Robert was beginning to retreat into himself and not be able to discuss and focus on the goals. He seemed tired and overwhelmed, which he was, but this was different. I tried to talk to him and discuss our plans, but he would just get agitated and not want to talk about it. He wasn't able to verbalize what was going on and try as I might, things just seemed to be going south. We disagreed more than usual and this cop of mine seemed to be losing ground. This spiraling downward was not what we had imagined for our time right after being out of the Force. We had wanted to spend some time away from home to help us adjust to life after the RCMP, but maybe this was a wrong decision. We worked hard and each day Bob seemed to get a little bit slower. He was tired I would tell myself, but Colin and I just kept on writing our goals down and striking them out at the end of each day. Each day Bob would need a little more down time even though he was still slugging away and accomplishing daily tasks. He was getting quieter and smiling less and I started worrying about my man.

The last weekend was a time crunch. Colin had renters moving in and the majority of the work was done. There were a few final touches to make, but basically this house was miraculously turned from a disaster zone into a cozy little bungalow. The night before the renters came in we celebrated our huge accomplishment. We had done it! Our son was set to enjoy his house with roommates and we could go home and recuperate.

Last Day of RCMP

Robert's holidays were used up quickly, and soon it was time for him to hand in his badge and actually finish his last final day of his RCMP career. He was ready and looking forward to not being a cop any longer. He hadn't missed the office or the work the last few months and had rested up from all the renovations. He seemed to have recuperated and our daily walking was helping him to recover again. He was now starting to worry about how we would handle making all our payments on his pension. We lived in a big house and how would we manage all of this? These were unusual worries for him. He had still been getting his regular paychecks up to this point, and soon this would end. We were used to getting paid biweekly, but his pension would come once a month. We would have to change our spending habits and adjust to only getting paid once a month. This would feel very strange after 35 years of being paid biweekly. We were both still young though and we could get a part-time job for extra income if we so desired, in fact, Robert had been offered some jobs already.

On July 23, 2014, Robert handed in his badge at the RCMP station in Williams Lake. He was only in the office for about an hour and came home quite excited. He was finished! He had accomplished his lifetime goal of achieving 35 years in the RCMP. For the most part, he had a career that he loved and he had finished well. We wanted to focus on the good and not the bad, so he was happy retiring as Sergeant in charge of Highway patrol for 3 units; Williams Lake, 100 Mile House and Quesnel. He managed 19 members during his time in Williams Lake and he enjoyed working alongside of them. He never expected them to do what he wasn't willing to do himself. He was well respected in the community and had fulfilled his commitment of serving 35 years in the RCMP. I was extremely proud of him for this huge accomplishment and that we had both survived the life of a cop. His 35-year pin would be handed out to him the following year via the Commissioner.

He handed in his badge and off we headed to Kelowna, where Kayce and Kevin were now living. They had asked if we would come and help them with their basement renovation and, of course, we were retired so we said we would. I knew Bob had been tired in Moose Jaw, but thought he had recovered and that he would be able to handle another work project to keep him occupied while adjusting to retirement.

It wasn't long before he seemed exhausted again and I could see him going downhill for a second time. This wasn't the cop I knew who could keep right on trucking with me. We went back and forth to Kelowna for the summer, doing a little more work each time, with camping trips in between to help us relax and enjoy a bit of down time with friends. The basement renovations were completed and ready for students to rent and now we could focus on ourselves. We made plans to travel to Arizona that fall with our truck and trailer and enjoy getting away and seeing some of the beautiful sights we wanted to visit. As we spoke about our trip and enjoyed planning it with our friends, the load became lighter and Robert seemed to pick up again.

Trip to Arizona

Our house was for sale, but there didn't seem to be much action in the housing market at this time. After retiring from the RCMP, our plan was to sell our house and move back to Kamloops, a place we still called home. We had loved our time in Kamloops and this was the city where our kids essentially grew up. It was home to them, so I guess that's why it was home to us. We talked to the realtor and he said to leave our house on the market while we were away on our trip to Arizona and he would call us if anything happened.

We packed up our truck and trailer and together, with our friends, we headed out of town for a month. We were ready for a holiday. My friend had breast cancer but she was feeling better than she had for a very long time. She was on a strict diet and following the advice of natural therapy. She was losing weight and could do more now than she had been able to do in years.

We were on our way to a Zija convention down in Utah, a network marketing company that we had both gotten involved in the previous year, and we were so looking forward to learning more about this great company and seeing the warehouses for ourselves. My friend had been hardly able to walk, but after using this product for only about six months she was able to wean herself off all her pain medication. Because of being on this great product, she went from hardly being able to walk to hiking Bryce Canyon with us!

We travelled down the United States down through Washington, Oregon, Utah and then into Arizona. We boon-docked along the way some nights and other nights we found interesting campsites to park at. We got to see some of the most beautiful sights we have ever seen including Bryce Canyon and the Grand Canyon. What amazing creations that takes your breath away and allows you to be filled with awe and wonder at the Creator. We had many highlights on our trip, but Bryce Canyon was a miraculous one for us. As we hiked down into the depth of this fairy tale land we couldn't help but give praise to the Creator who designed this special wonder of the world. It was totally awe-inspiring for the four of us. We kept asking my friend if she should turn around and go back up, but she kept on going down further and said she would make it back up. We will never forget that day and the smile on her face as she finished the hike. It was like a dream come true; she had accomplished a goal that she thought would never come to pass, and she was able to enjoy the majesty of this canyon with us. It was unbeatable.

We enjoyed so many days together. The Grand Canyon in its entire splendor was another attraction that took our breath away. Its grandeur is too hard to put into words; it is indescribable, incomprehensible, unfathomable and we are so fortunate to have been able to see it.

We had another wonderful experience in the little town of Williams, Arizona. We were looking for a place to eat and had pulled over to talk about where we should go. This tall guy with a big cowboy hat and a great big roll of bills stepped out of his pick-up truck and came over to ask us if he could help us. We told him that we were looking for a place to eat and he told us that the place right across the street, The Wild West Saloon, had the best food in town. He said that we could go to either place on each side and that they also had excellent food for twice the price, but that his place was the best food for the lowest price. After talking to him for a bit we decided to take him up on his offer. We went behind the saloon and entered into a beautiful little courtyard, a saloon-like old time historic town, and enjoyed a delicious meal together. The owner of the saloon had asked this band to come and play for the town one last time, as they were heading to Nashville the very next day to try and make it big. Then by a divine appointment we met up with a fellow who knew our friends. Years earlier on a ferry going to Vancouver Island, this man had asked our friends to pray for him and his boys as he was going through a difficult time. They recognized each other in the courtyard and we had a wonderful time catching up with what had happened since that ferry ride. If we hadn't taken the opportunity given to us that evening, we would have missed out on such a blessing on our vacation.

After the evening was over the tall guy with the big cowboy hat said that he would drive ahead of us and lead us to a campsite at the end of town so we could get there in the dark without difficulty. What a gentleman he was and it was a privilege to meet someone so helpful. As we said goodnight to this tall stranger we went into the office to register for our campsites and the staff asked us how we happened to know the Mayor of their little town of Williams, Arizona. We had quite the chuckle then, as he had been such a humble man, and we would never have known that he was the Mayor of Williams. What a blessing it was to have this whole spiritual experience so far away from home. The blessings are everywhere we look; we only have to just open our eyes to receive them. This was a little piece of heaven given to us and made me appreciate a little more of what my mom would be enjoying up there as well.

Our month on vacation flew by and soon we were saying goodbye to our friends again, only this time they were staying and we were heading home. We made the long trek back to British Columbia in four days. We had a fantastic holiday but now it was time to get back to reality. We needed to decide about our house, whether to sell it or take it off the market, and to decide what we were going to do with our lives if we stayed in Williams Lake. When retiring from the RCMP, members are given two years to sell their house and have the moving costs covered by the federal government. After two years we would have to cover this cost on our own. We needed to decide if we should take a loss on the house and move to Kamloops, or if we should stay in Williams Lake and retire there. I desperately wanted to move back to Kamloops, after all, our three lovely grandchildren were in Kamloops and we wanted to be around to see them grow up and be a part of their lives.

Selling Our House

We met with our realtor and discussed the possibility of taking our house off the market. He had earlier suggested that we leave it on the market until the end of October and then relist again in the spring. Robert and I spoke at length about this decision and we came to the conclusion that we would take it off the market and bunk down for the winter. We also had a meeting with another realtor in town, who was seemingly selling more properties than our realtor. She had the reputation of selling off things way too cheap, but at least she was selling properties. We wanted to know what she would say our house was worth so we set up a meeting with her.

Sure enough, we were shocked by what she told us to list for. No wonder her listings were selling. They were way lower than the other realtors in town, so of course, people selling with her were losing money, but people buying with her were getting a great deal. At least she was moving properties though; we had to give her credit for that. We told her that we had decided not to list for now but that we would list in the spring again. However, if she suddenly had someone interested in our house we would be willing to show it and sell through her.

That very next week we got a call from this realtor and she had someone interested in our house. Now we had some more big decisions to make. What was the bottom line that we would sell for? We knew what we had put into the house and what we wanted from the sale. However, in the current market value, what would be reasonable and did we really want to move right now? If so, then we needed to make a decision.

We ended up selling our house, losing some money, but we were financially better off getting rid of it and all the expenses that came with owning a big house on an RCMP pension. Robert had been worrying about how we were going to manage a big house so this seemed to be the right decision at the time. We could get out and move to where our grandkids were and buy a smaller place with lower living expenses. This was, after all, our plan for retirement, so all was coming to fruition. We should be ecstatic, so why weren't we?

How to Survive the Ride?

There is so much loss in life and it happens to all of us at one time or another. No one is exempt. It might be the loss of a job, the loss of a friendship, the loss of a missed opportunity, the loss of a miscarriage, the loss of a loved one, or the loss of the ability to carry on. The sun shines on the good and the bad and the rain pours on us all. However, how we deal with these downpours determines how fast the sun will come out to allow us to grow and blossom once again. To survive the ride, we must allow ourselves time to grieve in order to heal. There is a time for everything under the sun but through these times we need to look for some bright light, even if it is miles away, that will enable us to be thankful in every situation, regardless of how insignificant it seems. The more we are grateful, the more we will know what to be grateful for.

Chapter 9
Retirement Disaster

Downsizing

Our house sold at the end of October and we needed to be out of our house by the end of November. We only had a month to downsize but we had so many boxes to go through and so much to get rid of. We thought we would be doing this in the spring time, but our plans changed suddenly with the sale of our house. We now had more decisions to make. Did we want to rent, buy, or just travel around the country for a year? We had talked a lot about taking a year off and just travelling and living in our trailer. Bob had wanted to do this earlier, but as the time came for our house hunting trip, he was letting go of this dream and only able to focus on needing a place to call home. He needed a home base, somewhere to store his tools, a garage to tinker in, a place to feel secure. His life as he had known it for the last 35 years had changed drastically. This feeling of insecurity, being unsettled for Robert was strange; it was not really him talking, but I felt I needed to listen to him this time as he was really feeling agitated about it all.

We started to work through boxes and go through things that we weren't going to need any longer. We wanted to downsize because the two of us didn't need a big place to live in. We would have to downsize in Kamloops anyway, as house prices were a lot higher than in Williams Lake. Since we had taken quite a hit on our property in Williams Lake and our monthly income had gone down considerably, we would have to be careful what kind of place we purchased so that finances would not be too tight. We still wanted to enjoy the lifestyle we were used to without having to work full time at another job.

The week of our house hunting trip was not as desirable as we would have hoped it would be. This trip was paid for by the RCMP and so we were able to stay in a nice hotel and enjoy the hot tub in the evenings to relieve the stress of house hunting by day. During this week I realized that Robert was experiencing quite a lot of anxiety. He couldn't really make easy decisions about what to eat, and he couldn't think through the pros and cons rationally like we usually would do when buying a house. He only saw that we didn't have enough money and that we needed to be careful not to get in too deep.

We already did own a town house in Kamloops that we rented out as an investment property and our realtor told us about another one that was for sale right beside the one we already owned. The seller was motivated due to illness, so we thought we would have a look at it. The purpose in buying another town house would be to fix it up with the intention to turn around and sell it and hopefully make a bit of a profit. We had done this previously in our marriage so why shouldn't we do this again. We had the time to do the renovations now that we were retired and it would give us something to work on without a time pressure. We put in an offer and ended up purchasing the town house, right next door to the one we already owned. How advantageous was that! I was excited and knew that we could definitely make a profit, if and when we sold, after renovating this townhouse. We were being given a chance to make up for what we lost in Williams Lake, and for this we were very thankful.

Change in Plans

As we went home to finish downsizing and purging, Robert became more and more weary. He struggled to go through his garage. In fact, I didn't know if he would actually be able to get through this task. There were boxes that he hadn't even looked at in 35 years. I am not very sentimental about holding onto things, like a lot of women are, so I didn't have a lot of stuff to purge myself. It wasn't hard for me to declutter and get rid of stuff throughout the years. After all, it is just stuff! My mom always found it hard to part with her things and she was much more sentimental than I was. We often laughed about this because she would ask me to come over to help her get rid of stuff, but of course she would only get rid of a few things that I suggested and wouldn't be able to part with the rest.

After five days of struggling through all the stuff in the garage, Robert finally got through the boxes and ended up with about five pick-up loads of junk that he hauled to the dump, as well as about 5 pick-up loads of good stuff that went to the Salvation Army. When I say we downsized I mean we really did purge and get rid of about half of our household items. We still had plenty for the movers to pack up but our goal was to have all our household items fit into our town house without having to rent a storage unit.

The moving company arrived and the fun began. This move was easy for them; it only took them a day this time to pack up our house, when usually it would take them two full days. We had done well. We were ready to leave town and again needed to say our goodbyes. It was awfully hard to say goodbye to my friend struggling with cancer, but she felt well and we were only 3 hours away. It was always hard to leave our friends every place we lived, but we were happy to be moving closer to our grandkids and our retirement plan had always been to move back to Kamloops.

We moved into our little town house the beginning of December and I thought we were going to live happily ever after. This was a drastic change compared to our comfortable house in Williams Lake, but what happened next was something I never expected in a million years. Robert became increasingly more agitated and more anxious with each passing day. He started pacing at night and wasn't able to sleep. He said he felt like a caged animal and that he hated our town house. He thought we had made a terrible mistake and we shouldn't have moved here. He was having panic attacks and anxiety like never before. He mourned the loss of my mother, the loss of his job, the loss of our house, the loss of his friends, the loss of his identity, the loss of his pay check, the loss of his job, and the loss of self-worth. He thought he was a complete failure and didn't know how we were going to make it financially. He couldn't think logically and see that we would be alright. He thought we had no money, we couldn't do anything, and that life was basically over for us. He thought that he couldn't support me, that he was a bad husband and that he shouldn't have retired. He was spiralling downward into a pit of despair. He couldn't sleep, which was so unusual for him, and pacing night after night getting more and more tired made things that much worse. This was not the cop I had married or the husband I knew.

Christmas was just around the corner. Our kids were coming home for the holidays and Bob should have been excited, but instead he worried about everything. This was what we had hoped for, to be around our children and grandchildren, and yet this was all a disaster. I was like a broken record trying to show Robert that we would be okay. We had a good pension and things weren't as bad as he thought they were. We had savings in the bank and we would be just fine. Because Bob was unable to even go grocery shopping with me due to panic attacks, I ended up having to do all the Christmas shopping by myself, which should have been something we enjoyed doing together. It was a vicious circle. He was so anxious about everything, which prevented him from going out, and yet being cooped up inside was making him feel like a caged animal. He was having panic attacks throughout the day if there was too much noise, or if there were too many people around, or if the TV was on or if the radio was too loud. He had panic attacks if we talked about money and yet he had a one-track mind about money. This was getting so out of hand and I didn't know what to do.

We were doing all the things our doctor had told us to do but they weren't helping. I was still managing to drag him out for a walk almost daily, even though we had a foot of snow on the ground. The walks were peaceful and we would talk and pray while we walked and I would try to encourage him to see the beauty around us. We were eating healthy food and taking vitamins. He was doing what his doctor had told him to do regarding sleep habits. We were doing everything right but, everything was wrong.

I went for a walk alone one day and phoned my dad in tears. My husband was losing it and I didn't know what to do. This must be PTSD (post traumatic stress disorder), I told my father, but I couldn't cope much longer myself this way. My dad could relate to depression and the feeling of despair, having suffered a stroke 20 years previously, and then losing his wife; he was a listening ear for me. He decided to come and stay with us for a few weeks which was his way of trying to support me. He was still grieving the loss of his wife, my dear mother, and maybe we could help support each other. At least he got me out every day, either going for coffee, or lunch or just for a drive, and yet Bob could barely ever come out with us. He would try and come out some days but would have to leave shortly after sitting down for coffee because a panic attack would hit him. They would flare up at any given moment and he didn't know how to cope with this. The chatter and the noise of the hustle and bustle were too overwhelming for him and he would have to get up and go. My strong hubby who lived 35 years as a cop was now in bed for the most part of every day and very often in the fetal position crying like a baby. I didn't know how to help him or what to do. Nothing I said or did was working and things just couldn't carry on this way. I really felt like I wasn't going to survive this ride!

The night Robert was dreaming about suicide, I knew that I had to do something out of desperation. I knew of a psychologist in town who dealt with a lot of ex-RCMP members. I called him up in a panic asking if he could see Robert, and told him that I thought he was suffering from PTSD and that he was dreaming about suicide. He arranged to see him the following morning at 9 a.m. for which I was very thankful. Robert managed to drive himself to the appointment, which he insisted he was able to do. By the end of the 2 hours the psychologist called me and said that Robert needed to head up to the emergency department and that he would meet us there.

I was hesitant to go to the hospital and yet knew that we had to do something. I didn't want my husband in the psych ward, but if that's where he needed to be then that is what we would have to do. The psychologist wrote a very good letter indicating suicidal thoughts, which Robert was to give to the emerg staff at the hospital. After the doctor read the letter from the psychologist, we were seen by a health clinician who came in and asked Robert some questions. She told us that the emotions he was feeling were good emotions and that she didn't really feel he should go on any medication at this time. She did prescribe a sleeping pill, that would help break the sleep pattern he was in, and hoped that with getting some rest this would help his disposition. The psychologist and the clinician explained adrenaline depletion to us. Being in the RCMP for 35 years and not having the adrenaline levels able to reach baseline before another spike would take place had taken its toll on Robert. Now, after a period of rest, with Robert just having retired his adrenaline levels were coming down without the spikes and he was experiencing adrenaline depletion. This definitely was going to take some time to recover. The clinician felt he should try to get some rest and keep seeing the psychologist to talk about all the traumatic events and incidents that he had witnessed in the last 35 years. We left the hospital with a prescription for a sleeping pill but with no other medication. I was relieved and yet weary. I was thankful he wasn't admitted and that the clinician felt he was stable.

The following five days on the sleeping pill were some of the worst yet. The pill did manage to break his sleep pattern somewhat and allowed him to sleep in his own bed for a little while each night. But during the day his panic and anxiety attacks escalated to about once every 30 minutes. He was literally curled up in bed, crying like a baby, and I would hold him and try to console his very being to the core. Still, this wasn't helping. I researched the medication he was taking and, sure enough, one of the side effects was anxiety. No wonder he was getting worse! I threw those pills in the garbage and wondered what we would do next.

Our life was not supposed to be like this. We were retired and were supposed to be enjoying this year. Not only did he hate it back in Kamloops, he also couldn't do anything to help his situation. He couldn't work if he had to. He was so worried about money and not having enough of it, but when he would search for jobs online he could only focus on not having the skills needed for the job. Even if he had a job, his anxiety and his panic attacks were so debilitating he couldn't have gone to work. If we wanted any extra money then I would have to be the one to earn it. I was actually still working online doing medical transcription, so the little extra income I made helped to ease his anxiety a little bit. I started looking for jobs outside the home now as well because I needed to get out of the house for my own sanity. I needed to be around some positive energy and start taking care of myself, which meant getting away from Robert for part of every day.

Robert went back to see the psychologist and we owe a lot to this man. He wrote a letter to our doctor stating that Robert wasn't getting any better and that he really needed to be on an antidepressant for a while. Sometimes the brain just can't heal without some medical intervention and this was one of those times. The psychologist diagnosed Robert with operational stress injury (or PTSD) for which he would need some help. He explained that it was an injury that would take time to heal, but that there would always be a scar.

Since this condition had come tumbling down after Robert had left the RCMP and he had not been diagnosed before retiring, he did not have any coverage through Veteran Affairs to help with the psychology visits or medication costs. The cost of a psychology visit was stressing Robert out so much that he said he didn't want to go, even though he knew he needed to go. The psychologist recognized this and said not to worry about paying for visits for the time being and that he would fight for Robert to get covered by Veteran Affairs. He filled out some forms and assured us that he would do what he could and that no one he had ever applied for had been rejected. This alleviated some of our fears, although there was always the chance of not being eligible for coverage. After a few visits to the psychologist, Robert was beginning to feel that he would eventually get better and realized that a lot of members suffer from operational stress injury; he was not alone in this.

Our GP prescribed Robert some medication and this was another game we had to play. Bob is very sensitive to medication so we knew this would be a trial and error type of game. Antidepressants have many side effects and, with being so sensitive, it was no wonder that he was affected by these medications. One medication made him as high as a kite where he was seeing very vivid translucent colours. Another one gave him such vertigo that he couldn't lift his head off the pillow; he barely made it to the washroom to vomit. He needed help with walking because he was so dizzy; he was like a man highly intoxicated. At one point I caught him from falling down a flight of stairs due to his dizziness, making me relive the nightmare of my mom's horrific fall. The game was challenging.

We tried five different medications and he ended up taking the lowest dose of one that wore off by evening, but that was all he could take. He could feel that it helped his mood and that it lifted his spirit a little bit, only he just didn't feel good physically on it. He persisted on this medication for 6 weeks at which time his muscles were aching too much to continue taking it, another side effect, and he eventually just wouldn't take it anymore. He was on the mend slowly with the medication but what would happen now that he went off of it? He did promise to restart it if I found him getting worse again. Maybe life would never be normal again and this was all we had to look forward to.

Survival at A&W

I met a man working at A&W while having coffee with my Dad there one day. He was around my age and in training, so we started a conversation. Through our conversation I learned that he was opening his own A&W very soon and that he would be hiring soon too. He told me to go and apply and that I should tell the interviewer that he had sent me. I had worked in the fast food industry before and always loved it. This would allow me to engage in something that would energize me and the little bit of extra money would be a bonus, but mostly it would be good for me to get out of the house and be around some positive people.

I was hired and the training and experience was a balm to my soul. I was working with teenagers and a few other people my age, but I loved the atmosphere and I could laugh and be myself without anyone knowing my real story at home. It was my escape from reality for the time being. How odd, I thought, that I had to resort to working at a fast food place to allow myself to heal and become encouraged. However, this was the best thing I could have done for myself. I looked forward to going to work and the challenge was stimulating for me. I had fun and was fulfilled while I was there making other people happy while doing my job. I would come home happy after an 8-hour shift and walk in the door to utter gloom. It was like walking from light into darkness, from beauty into ashes, from life into death. It was a heaviness that I cannot explain.

Pressing On With or Without You

Robert and I still talked about things even when he was depressed. I tried to stay positive and keep up the communication with him, right or wrong. I was going to move on with my life because I just couldn't live this way anymore. This didn't mean that I was leaving him; it meant that I was going to take care of myself or I wouldn't be able to look after him. He understood this and certainly didn't want my life to be this way. It was hard for me to say things to him because I didn't want to make him feel worse, but I needed to let him know that I was not going to live in his world of fear nor would I listen to depressing conversation all the time.

My daughter, Kayce, and I had always wanted to own a coffee shop together. This had been a dream of ours for a very long time. Throughout the past 5 years we had looked at a few shops that were for sale, but we never felt the peace we needed to follow through and buy one. We had put in an offer on a little shop two years previously, but at the time she had become pregnant and wanted to be a stay-at-home mom, as well as my mom was suffering from Alzheimer's, so we dropped pursuing it further.

Kayce called me one day to let me know that she had been searching for businesses for sale and, lo and behold, the same coffee shop we had wanted to buy two years earlier was for sale again. A new door was opening and this was a new beginning for us. We started pursuing this sale, regardless of the state my husband was in, and discussions and meetings were held.

Like I said before, I kept communicating with Robert, good or bad, right or wrong, so I told him about the coffee shop as well. We had a lot of discussion around the purchase of the shop and how the fears would hold him back, but that I was an entrepreneur at heart and that I needed to follow my dreams after allowing him his career in the RCMP. He encouraged me to pursue my dream regardless of whether he was anxious about money. He wanted me to move forward even if we had to have meetings without him. I was thankful for his support even though he was so nervous about it all. We talked about our financial affairs and how this would affect us if we went under in this endeavour. We talked about the best case scenarios and the worst case scenarios; we listed the pros and cons. We had some savings to fall back on and we had Bob's pension so we would be fine either way, we knew we would be able to survive this ride with its ups and downs.

So the decision was made to press on and pursue this new career for Kayce and I, with or without Robert, but in my heart I knew it was the best decision for us both because it would help him heal both physically, mentally and give him a purpose again. His sense of identity would return through the social aspect and the sense of ownership of something. He needed to feel useful and worthwhile once more and this whole retirement sentiment needed to vanish.

The next months were filled with meetings about buying the coffee shop, mulling over the financial reports, meeting with lawyers, going into the coffee shop to watch and observe whether we wanted to keep the current staff or hire new staff, trying different menu items to see what we would want to keep and what we would want to change, all the while not disclosing that we were interested in buying the business. This was exciting and a little unnerving, yet we kept plunging forward. The day came when we made the final decision – we were buying!

Losing a Best Friend

My good friend in Williams Lake was going downhill. The cancer was starting to take over her body and she was getting tired and run down. Her health was being snatched away very quickly. We had seen our friends in April just before they headed down south for a month of hot weather, and before she left I told her that she shouldn't lose any more weight. She was starting to look unhealthy and her vivacity was waning. After being gone for a month, they stopped in to see us again on their way home and this time she really didn't look well. She was getting scared and didn't know what to do. She didn't want to go to the doctor, but knew she needed some help because she couldn't cope with the pain in her breast and chest much longer. We cried and laughed and I supported her every decision. She had decided to go the holistic route and whether people agreed with her or not, this was her decision. She was happy with her decision and so I was happy with her as well. She believed in natural medicine and truly believed that she would be healed, so being a close friend I supported her through this.

After being home for just a few weeks she started to fade and get very weak. She was hospitalized at the end of May and by the middle of June my friend was taken from this life. She always thought she would be healed, but was now in a better place up in heaven and in this way she was healed. I was fortunate enough to visit her in the hospital a few times and I was also able to say goodbye and be there when she passed. When someone important is taken from us we tend to consider what is truly important to us. Material things don't matter to a dying person, but forgiveness and mending broken relationships are at the forefront. My friend had a heart of gold; she was a gem who loved people and didn't judge a soul. She held all my secrets in her heart and now she was gone.

I had lost my mom; I had lost my husband emotionally for almost a year; and now my very dear friend was gone. I wasn't surviving the ride too well at the moment.

Leaning on Faith

Faith had become a big part of our lives throughout the ride so it was no wonder that I would cry out to God at a time like this. I know that there is a plan for my life and taking the opportunities that are given to me are a big part of the plan. Stepping out in faith is not always easy day after day. I knew that the PTSD journey with this cop of mine was going to be a long road, and I knew I had to cling to my faith and take one day at a time. He was getting better, slowly but surely, and I could see he was making headway and clearing through some of the fog. I needed him more than ever now and longed for him to be there to share my joys and sorrows alongside of me. I was quite a strong woman but for months now I would lay my head on the pillow at night and cry myself to sleep. Tears are healing and silent and usually the mornings looked brighter. In the back of my mind I knew that God was allowing us to go through this journey so that we would be able to help others go through their journey. Experiencing hardship makes you either give up on your faith or makes it stronger, and mine was made stronger.

How to Survive the Ride?

I found that learning how to survive the ride was too difficult without a higher power to lean on. My faith kept me going through the big and the little things throughout my life. Some people say it's just a crutch but I say it's much more than that. It is a personal relationship that allows me to confide in my Maker and cry out to Him in my frustrations as well as my triumphs and receive healing to my soul. It's a source of light in a dark world that keeps me going and fills my life with purpose. We all go through ups and downs in our lives and have to be ready to change the trajectory of our course along the way at times. It is realizing when we need to change and be ready to make those changes which enables us to move forward easier. My God was with me one step at a time, one day at a time, one ride at a time and my faith held on and grew stronger throughout the ride.

Chapter 10
The Future Looks Bright

The Coffee Shop

We had made the big decision to move forward with the Coffee Shop and things were going crazy. People told me I was crazy, but I already knew that. They thought I was doing the wrong thing with Robert being sick, but I kept telling people I knew it would help him get better. He was getting better and this would help him recover even more. He was now able to get out a little bit and focus on a conversation somewhat. The decisions for the shop were made mostly without him, even though he was a part of the company. He still couldn't discuss financial details in depth because he would get into a panic mode about money too quickly. While he was ill, fixating on finances was such a trap for him so we tried to avoid having these conversations around him, if we could.

The week before we took over the business we met with all the staff and let them know that we were the new owners. We were excited to get started and the first month we would just come in and observe as the staff worked and carried out their daily tasks. We were lucky to have the staff stay on with us, as most customers are very loyal to their service people. The first week we made a lot of contacts and met a lot of regular customers. We let our customers know that we were the new owners and that we were there to serve them and make their experience in the coffee shop a good one. Some people were receptive to this while others were not; change is very hard for some people. Loyalty is a funny thing in business; we had to earn the respect of our customers, which we knew would take time, but we also knew that with a bit of time they would come to like us and shift their loyalties to us.

We made little changes here and there and tried to be patient so that the loyalty shift would take place. We are all creatures of habit, so changing a coffee shop can be a bit daunting. We certainly didn't want to lose our regular customers. I remember the day when we felt the change. Suddenly we were the accepted new owners and we would now be able to make some bigger changes. Our customers had learned to trust us and we were on our way to success. We were having fun serving people and giving back to the community.

We needed to build up the business and we were working night and day to make a go of it. We had goals and aspirations about the shop before we purchased it, so we worked hard to reach these goals. One of our main goals was to jump in and start a business somewhere then, once we had mastered a small one, we would jump into something bigger. My daughter and I are entrepreneurs at heart and without realizing our dreams our purpose in life would not come to pass. We are told to dream big and that we are only as big as we dream, so we have dreamt big!

One Step at a Time

While working in the coffee shop, we have met other entrepreneurial business people who are like minded which is totally refreshing to us. Having an open mind and thinking outside of the box is extremely hard for many people. Having a mastermind group to meet with is a worthwhile endeavour whether it is on the phone or actually meeting in person. I am so fortunate to have a friend who I chat with, on the phone, frequently who is of kindred spirit and also thinks like me, outside the box. We met through circumstances that I could never have orchestrated myself, and if I hadn't taken the opportunity that presented itself to me years ago with Zija, the network marketing company, I would never have met this beautiful woman. We don't live in the same city but we share a connection that goes deep. Being able to share ideas with each other and not be ridiculed for our big dreams is encouraging for both of us. Everyone needs a good mentor and friend to keep you accountable and help you reach your potential.

My retired cop was definitely on the mend. His mental clarity was coming back and he was able to focus on tasks again. His self-worth was returning and he was now able to see that he still had a lot to offer. He had applied for a few jobs and was now able to pick from a variety of positions, which increased his self-confidence also. He was now able to continue consulting in the trucking industry, which he had begun just before he got sick. During his 35 years in the RCMP he had been the commercial vehicle coordinator for approximately 10 years, along with being a commercial vehicle safety alliance inspector for close to 20 years. With this knowledge he was able to do consulting in the commercial truck industry, as well as teaching and assessing driver skills for companies with fleets. The coffee shop had done what I had hoped it would do for him and for this I will be forever grateful for my persistence in stepping forward to make this dream a reality. Robert was able to sit and have coffee with a group of regular customers in the mornings who accepted him for who he was, sick or otherwise, and the sense of ownership gave him a feeling of accomplishment and fulfillment after retiring from the RCMP. Every day I could see him improving. His joy was returning as he had a reason to get up in the morning. Even though we were working very long tiring days, the reason to get up was what he needed. He was sleeping better, his psychologist said he was improving, and although the injury that took place in his brain was still there, he was learning how to cope and live with it. Operational stress injury is something that can heal, but there will always be a scar; the scar fades, but never goes away. The shop was a center for healing for which I will be forever grateful, regardless of whether we made any money. It is always one day or one step at a time because we don't know what each day will hold for us.

Winter Wonderland

As we headed into another winter season we believed it was actually going to be fun celebrating Christmas in the coffee shop this year. Robert was doing so much better than the last year and we were thankful to actually enjoy spending time with family and friends. We were taking a few days off over the Christmas holidays, but we were working longer hours. We had booked some extra Christmas functions in the evenings, as well as working in the coffee shop during the day. Working hard was a positive thing compared to the previous year with Robert being so sick and in bed. Being physically tired and falling asleep at night is truly a gift. We take these little blessings in life for granted and we don't realize how precious the simple things in life are until they are gone. A year ago, Robert hadn't been able to sleep and would be up pacing night after night. Now he was putting his head on the pillow after a day at the shop and would be asleep in a flash. A year ago I felt like I was going into one of the darkest, most troubling times of my life with a cop, and as I reflect back now it feels like a dream. In the dark time, it was like looking into a cloudy, misty mirror with only just a tiny spot in the center where I could barely see myself. Eventually, as the darkness faded, the mist receded and was only around the outer edges of the mirror. As the darkness lifted, my life transformed again. It was like waking up to a fresh new beautiful snowfall. The world was a winter wonderland with pure crystal snowflakes enticing me to reach out and touch them. This new enticement was going to replace the void of the last year and this new beginning would be pure and fresh like the snowflakes, a real winter wonderland.

Thinking Outside of the Box

So many people are raised in a society of thinking that your life consists of the following: you are born, go to school, go to university, get a good job, work for 35 plus years and if you're lucky have a good pension, retire and finally do what you want to do. Life is so much more than this. Life is about living every day to your full potential and discovering what your passion is, and then achieving your goals to fulfill your purpose. We too thought that we had to finish off 35 years with the RCMP so that we would receive a good pension. It wasn't until we went to a life changing conference that helped us realize that we needed to think outside of the box and change our way of thinking. Life is full of opportunities that come our way, we just have to reach out and take them and when we change our way of thinking we can make things happen. Since we have begun to think outside of the box, numerous opportunities have come our way.

Just Around the Corner

Throughout the years, Robert and I have always dreamt big. Some people thought we were absolutely ridiculous but others accepted us for the crazy couple we were. We were the most unlikely people to ever meet, unless you believe in divine appointments. Robert was from a little town in Newfoundland and I was from a small town in British Columbia. We grew up 5000 miles apart and yet we met, fell in love, and spent a life time learning and maturing into the people we are today. Some people would call this fate but I call it divine intervention. I am so thankful for the life I am living and being able to share it with Robert. I look forward to living a little bit more every day, waking up a little bit more every day, and thinking outside the box a little bit more every day. We are entering another phase of life which is just like going around another corner. We can't see what is around the corner until we actually turn into it. Some corners are sharp and harder to turn which demand a bit more grip on the wheel, while others are longer and smoother, requiring less of a grip on the wheel. I am looking forward to what is just around the corner because with every turn there is something different to learn. Life is always an adventure no matter what phase we are in, and we are looking forward to the next ride of our life now.

Endless Roads to Ride

I am excited about what lies ahead for Robert and I. Yes, we have had challenges that knocked us down for a time, but most people have faced some sort of challenge that required time to get their feet back on the ground. These hard knocks have made us stronger people and given us a different outlook on life. We try not to take things for granted now like sleep, good health, and the ability to think clearly. These are blessings not to be overlooked. We have so much more we want to accomplish and many more experiences we want to share. As we celebrate the victory of overcoming our struggles, it is our desire to help others who also face some of the same challenges in their lives. We hope that sharing our experiences will encourage others in their journey and help them overcome the obstacles in their path.

Robert and I are more focused on things we want to pursue now than ever before. We are not retired, but refired! We can see so many opportunities now and want to reach out and explore them. I think the more we learn and grow, the more we want to learn and grow. The opportunities are endless; we just have to see the ones in front of us and choose which ones we want to take. There are endless roads to ride that can take you many different directions. Choosing which road to take is the first step in starting the ride of your life. The possibilities are endless and the future looks bright.

How to Survive the Ride?

The future is bright and we are not only surviving the ride but we are enjoying the ride. It is important to enjoy the ride you are on, even though at times it will be bumpy. Surviving isn't always fun but we still had fun along the way. Life is a roller coaster of emotions and being able to ride the storms of life with an attitude of gratitude is a valuable tool that carries you from one ride to the next.

Robert and I have been together now for almost 34 years and we hope to have many more exciting, fun-filled years together. Supporting one another, believing in each other and having fun together are essential in surviving the ride. Robert and I have done this together and I can honestly say I have loved My Life With A Cop.

Made in the USA
Charleston, SC
28 April 2016